The 14 Karmic Laws of Love: How to Develop a Healthy and Conscious Relationship With Your Soulmate

Dan Desmarques

Published by 22 Lions Bookstore, 2019.

Table of Contents

Copyright Page 1

About the Publisher 3

Introduction 5

How to Recognize Your Karmic Relationships 7

Why Your Soulmate Can Be a Stubborn Soul 11

How to Identify a Karmic Connection Within You 13

How Your Spiritual State Influences Your Soulmate 15

The Meanings Behind the Emotional Chaos 17

The Importance of Accepting Your Soulmate 19

Why People Reject Their Soulmate 21

How to Recognize Behavior Patterns in a Soulmate 23

How I Found a Great Soulmate 25

How to Accept Your Karmic Challenges 29

How to Overwrite Your Fear Patterns 33

Why Faith in Your Karmic Path is So Important 35

The Importance of Your Decisions 39

The Connection Between Desires and Reincarnations 41

The Self-Deceptive Path of the Personality 43

How Karma Emerges From Emotional Connections 45

The Relationship Between Reincarnation and the Ego 47

The Countries Where You Should Look for a Soulmate 49

The Challenges of the Most Developed Souls	51
Why Do People Fear Believing in Past Lives?	53
Why Do We Allow Our Fears to Destroy Our Dreams?	55
Why Do We Need to Confront Our Karmic Cycles?	57
The Influence of Karma in Our Spiritual Purpose	59
Why Love Reappears in a New Life	61
Why Relationships Between Soulmates Fail	67
When Two Soulmates Have a Quarrel	71
Why Karma Destroys Relationships	79
Why We Allow The Past to Repeat Itself	83
Why Soulmates are Usually Different Individuals	87
The Mental Battle Between Soul and Society	89
The Transition Between Our Emotional Dilemmas	91
Why Do We Repeat The Same Stories	95
The Importance of Sex Between Soulmates	97
The Spiritual Consequences of Promiscuity	99
The Meaning of Reincarnation in Our Personal Life	101
Why are People Irresponsible about their Karma	103
How Many Types of Relationship Exist?	105
Why Most People Can't Change?	109
How To Accept Love Between Soulmates?	113
Understanding Karmic Love Between Soulmates	117

The Third Hidden Element in All Relationships 121

When and Who Should We Forgive? 125

Who Deserves Love the Most? 127

The Soulmates You Can't Accept 131

How Do People Make Themselves Suffer 133

Karma and the Obsession with Manipulation 137

The 14 Karmic Laws of Love 139

Copyright Page

The 14 Karmic Laws of Love: How to Develop a Healthy and Conscious Relationship With Your Soulmate

By Dan Desmarques

Copyright © Dan Desmarques, 2019 (1st Ed.). All Rights Reserved.

Copyright © Dan Desmarques, 2019 (2nd Ed.). All Rights Reserved.

Published by 22 Lions Bookstore and Publishing House

About the Publisher

About the 22 Lions Bookstore:

www.22Lions.com

Facebook.com/22Lions

Twitter.com/22lionsbookshop

Instagram.com/22lionsbookshop

Pinterest.com/22lionsbookshop

Introduction

Most people go through life without understanding the purpose of their existence or how their past reincarnations keep affecting their decisions and emotions in the present time, and even interfering with the dynamics of their relationships.

Although we don't necessarily always find someone we met in a previous life, it is a fact that, due to our predisposed energy field and the way it is arranged, we tend to always be drawn towards those with whom we have an emotional connection with, and for good or for worse. That connection tends to find reasons within our karmic path.

As you can see, one way or another, we are attracted to what is beautiful or broken. But the outside is always a reflection of the inside, and both elements of reality complement one another. The physical world is nothing but the theatre of our spiritual manifestations and learnings.

Indeed, there are different reasons behind our many behaviors and thoughts, most of which are much older than we want to believe. The physical aspect of them is nothing but a form of justification within a wider spectrum related to our own eternal growth.

The more you understand this and learn to actually see it, the faster you will be in learning how to make proper decisions towards your most desired outcomes.

In this book, you will gain a better perception of how karma affects your life, and how previous reincarnations affect the way you think. You will also learn how to clean your karma, how to find your soulmate, and how to keep a healthy relationship with someone you have met in another life.

Ultimately, the path that is unveiled here, will guide you in finding your true self, while identifying the traits that can make you a better person.

Most likely, what makes this book completely unique, among so many others on this topic, is that while it was being written, it was also happening to the author himself. Basically, the author found a soulmate during the editing process and decided to include here an in-depth analysis of the story, to help his readers in understanding the topic with a pragmatic and honest approach to it, and without occulting any personal aspects.

The parallel between the theory, the analysis, and the reality, will guide you towards finding real love in the most comprehensive way possible.

How to Recognize Your Karmic Relationships

We don't really understand why certain people appear in our life despite the way we feel about them, even when our brain tells us that they don't match how we see ourselves.

Many times, such individuals show a completely unexpected appearance, skin color, tone of voice or anything else that just doesn't seem to resemble anyone we ever met before in our current existence. And yet, somehow, they feel familiar to us.

That which intrigues us, propels our curiosity towards them, and by following through, we become entangled in their reality.

From that point on, we can't really avoid either the conflicts, the misinterpretations, the chaotic thoughts, the frustrations or contradictions, and everything else that occurs within us and in between. Although the biggest challenge typically occurs when they present a willingness towards a direction we have once had but do not wish to see in a lifetime partner.

If you ever found yourself thinking about someone you had just met for no particular reason, that was most likely a symptom of an encounter with a soulmate, or at the very least, someone you have met before, in another life.

The most interesting thing about such encounters, it the delusional idea that most people have that they can somehow avoid the consequences. Because you can deny the impact it has on you, but you can't really avoid it. You can choose what you wish to do with fate but you can't stop it.

Due to my level of consciousness, I can easily tell who is supposed to meet me for karmic reasons. Sometimes I talk to them about those reasons and sometimes I don't, depending on how much they seem prepared to handle the truth.

Many of those who can't get any answers from me, often call me mysterious and claim that I have a high ability to avoid questions, but that is not something that I do on purpose. It is rather a natural behavior and adjustment coming out of an analysis that I do on their soul, and that proves itself accurate every single time.

There are also occasions in which I do the opposite, by either ridiculing my level of awareness, devaluing the amount of knowledge I possess, or by ignoring the conceptualizations others have formed about themselves. And I do that for the same reasons.

Not always the one who is not prepared is the one who lacks the knowledge. There are also many situations in which the one with the most knowledge has trapped himself in his own beliefs, and in doing so, delayed his own spiritual growth.

This situation is actually very common among very religious individuals. I have seen many examples of this in Freemasonry and Rosicrucianism. And I must say that, those in these groups who have shown fear and resentment towards me, are precisely the ones who need me the most.

Human beings get confused and lost for different motives, being the most common, the following:

- An erroneous sense of self-importance;

- Misinterpreted or misleading information;

- The incapacity to adjust to contradictory beliefs;

- The fear to change towards new paradigms.

Not only is irrelevant to discuss deeper topics with such people, but also dangerous.

THE 14 KARMIC LAWS OF LOVE

It is for this reason that I advise my students of cartomancy to never disclose everything that they see in a reading. Not before, at least, making a proper judgement on how much responsibility the other person can take. Otherwise, the effect of a good intention may very well be a negative result.

Not many people can understand this, despite how intelligent they may seem.

I was once invited to discuss my knowledge about karma in Lithuania and refused. The people in the group kept insisting that they were very interested in hearing me speak about the topic and others that I also write about in my books. But I kept refusing. And they couldn't understand why.

After they repeatedly asked me why, I answered:

— "I don't think most of the people attending one of my public presentations will be prepared for what I will tell them. The effects may vary and are very unpredictable."

One of them, coincidentally a psychologist, said:

— "You can't be responsible for what others do with what you give them."

With this answer, she actually justified me, because I was talking about them. In other words, if they are so irresponsible about what they learn, they deserve to learn nothing from me.

That answer, in the form of a projection, quite clearly, verbalized what I could see.

The same applies to the topic of soulmates. You can't really discuss it, no matter how obvious it may seem to you, or how much you need someone else to trust you.

This, unless the other person in front of you is ready to accept his lack of control over his own fate. Because, quite often, the response of someone confronted with this topic is exactly the opposite of what you would expect or want.

Basically, he or she will suppress what they fear to confront, by exercising a stronger control over their own reality. And even if that control is delusional, it means avoiding the one claiming to be a soulmate.

The more you prove yourself right, the more you will scare the other person away.

For the vast majority of mankind, the only way to fulfill their karma and attract a soulmate, is by actually not knowing anything about it, and remain arrogantly stupid.

I have learned this lesson the hardest way, by telling previous girlfriends, whom in some cases were indeed soulmates, that they would be deceived into leaving my life for karmic reasons, upon finding a man with whom they would betray me, even if that relationship wouldn't last. Apparently, and based on the outcome, in their brain, they understood something like: "He is trying to stop me from finding my real soulmate."

You see, even with this knowledge in hands, you still have to be careful when dealing with a soulmate, before and during a relationship. And being skillful in the art of managing emotions is something that shows itself crucial for your own success.

Why Your Soulmate Can Be a Stubborn Soul

Whatsoever is what I do with the soulmates I encounter, I always observe an extremely high level of arrogance that blinds them to the obvious. That obvious, tends to be disguised as a very strong layer of emotions that appear to have the same characteristics as love.

Another interesting element about this type of love, is that it awakens the greatest fears of the soul. It would be the equivalent to an atheist woman falling in love for a very religious man, or a very independent woman falling in love with a very dominant man, or a very insecure person falling in love with a very confident one, or a woman without self-esteem falling in love with someone who admires her, and so on.

People runaway from that which awakens their deepest fears. When confronted with the option between fear and love, they pick fear. It's easier. But in doing so, they also delay their own spiritual progress.

Such people assume that they are running away from a certain individual, while in fact they are running away from themselves.

Love and fear are both opposites on the same emotional scale, and they only appear at the same time when there is a spiritual lesson to be confronted.

You won't get a soulmate as someone that matches you in every way. That's a mental perspective of the topic in which many want to believe, because most human beings are mental creatures, and not spiritual or emotional. They want to understand reality and live it based on their beliefs, even if such beliefs are, to a great extent, completely artificial and self-fabricated.

This is just the way it is, because that's how they manifest their karma. Karma is nothing more than the exercise of beliefs. And that is why karma is always self-imposed.

We may say that it is convenient to consider a soulmate as someone who matches our thoughts and ambitions in life, someone that, somehow, resembles our cultural background and accepts it. But that's not a soulmate! That's a self-delusional mate, someone who has embraced the same ignorance that we share.

If such was true, it would be the same as being in an asylum to be treated for psychopathy and end up falling in love with another psychopath.

Most human beings, because they are insane, think of love in such insane way. And it is not surprising that the movie industry, and the many novels out there, cater exactly to the demand, therefore reinforcing, in the name of profit and popularity, the same beliefs.

It is always a grave danger, when certain individuals, in an anxious need for fame and riches, seek to hijack the minds of the many, for in doing so, they predispose themselves to the influences of the dark side of the spiritual world, desperately seeking the same, but for other, more devastating reasons.

Those who need recognition the most, are the ones who should get it the least, for in their despair to obtain it, they will do anything for it, and reduce their consciousness along the way before any sense of responsibility for the fate of others.

The need to put oneself ahead and before any development of attributes and the natural necessity to provide value to the world, is a demonstration of immaturity and lack of consciousness in what regards the mechanics of life. And the many who have gone down this road, will eventually realize that they are heading in the wrong direction.

How to Identify a Karmic Connection Within You

We must always suspect that which feels too good to be true, because it often is.

The laws of the planet simply don't allow anything without a certain sequence of events, at which the primordial level is sacrifice.

Now, in what regards the topic of this book, I am talking about the sacrifice of the soul, in the form of the burning of the personality to the fire of consciousness. In other words, you must see and experience in order to confront your fears, if you want to know true love. There is no other way.

As mentioned previously, one of the things that I came to realize about interactions with soulmates, is that, when you are in the presence of one of such souls, you feel a strong connection, but it's not necessarily a positive feeling.

The way you feel about them also doesn't mean that they are bad people, but only that there is a certain chemistry being triggered by a past life memory.

We naturally tend to assume that, when an emotion towards someone is negative, that has to do with evil, and that such individual has done something bad to us before, reason why we feel this way. We then consider that our reactions towards such person are justified. However, our brain has a way to deceive us, for logical reasons.

As a matter of fact, those who have done evil to others in a past existence are more likely to feel such fear, in the form of the fear of exposure. And so, they tend to repeat the previous karma in the same way.

Besides, contrary to what you might have been told, the purpose of your brain is not to help you spiritually, but to preserve your body. The brain operates as a very basic, and often stupid, mechanism.

To think that your brain is all you need to make proper conclusions about your interactions, is to reduce your existence to the level of any animal in a farm. And yes, I say it correctly, animal in a farm. Because your own thinking and living, and any decisions that you make along the way, will be confined to the thinking and living system of the masses, of those who surround you and affect you at an emotional level.

With such paradigm in you, you will be a slave to your own thoughts without even realizing it. And when this happens, your spiritual evolution is slowed to such an extent, that you might as well be frozen in time.

You must know as well that, the more this occurs, the more likely you are to die. Because, for mysterious reasons, the body always responds to the state of the spirit. And so, it is not the mind that controls it, but the spiritual state of your being.

How Your Spiritual State Influences Your Soulmate

The more we neglect our spiritual nature, the more the contrast between the state of awareness and consciousness increases. From that point on, we seem to become too stupid in avoiding even that which the brain should be good at noticing, i.e., accidents, conflicts and the probability of death.

Anyone who is developing self-destructive habits is already, somehow, manifesting what I just said. And so, as absurd as it may seem, those who do not care about what they eat and drink, those who do not care about whom they associate themselves with, those who hurt the ones who love them, those who neglect the need for compassion and empathy, and those who engage in sexual behaviors of risk, as when having sex with strangers they barely know, are all, and despite social beliefs and norms, participating in a degradation of the spirit, while conducting themselves to a faster death, as if, in actuality, seeking it.

The lack of capacity to differentiate what brings one upwards or downwards in life itself, makes people completely unconscious to the meaning of their existence. The comprehension of the karmic laws then remains as a topic too far from their reach.

Within such gap, they find the many authors and books, and idiotic life coaches, that pull them further downwards.

It's actually very easy to trap a lost soul based on the lack of insights about spirituality. After all, how do you know in whom to trust, if you lack the basics to make such distinction?

The common and natural behavior of the masses in this aspect is to trust themselves. I.e., to focus on what the masses are already doing, by following trends, recommendation of friends, what is popular, and so on. And how convenient this is, for it drives them towards the worse, and what they should't actually read or accept.

Now, we may question ourselves, if it is worse to find an author influenced by demonic forces or to remain stupid and learn on our own, but either way, is not a real way.

At the very least, we should always learn the basics of how to think effectively, and most people lack such basics.

I am always curious about what the masses seek, in order to study the why, but I do have the mental and spiritual skills to discern such individuals and their own work. And well, every time I investigated the most praised authors, and their public speakings, I found them to be terrible. Or better said, great at manipulating the masses towards their own self-degradation and spiritual self-destruction.

The large majority of the population is so asleep, that they can't even see how many popular authors trap their mind in thinking patterns that guide them into a quicker state of self-destruction. And they can't see it, precisely because they already trust too much of their own thinking process. It would be the equivalent to an investment on a wider form of stupidity because it matches its minor form.

The sense of familiarity propels many to their condemnation, in an anxious attempt to end suffering by what appears to be a salvation. And so, the problem is not as much in the wolves in sheep's clothing as it is in the idea that humans are just sheep. Because, when you degrade yourself through the wrong self-conceptualizations, you also take the exact same thinking structure that identifies you with those conceptualizations.

The Meanings Behind the Emotional Chaos

The vast majority of the population is not aware of their own past lives, and that's why they typically lose the benefits of encountering the soul of someone they have met before.

Most even believe that we evolve alone and don't need to change. But people do change, even when they don't want to.

All of our conflicts and encounters, no matter how much resentment or tears have caused us, or how much they lasted in time, have something to teach us, quite often more about ourselves than the encounter itself or the other person.

You see, the importance of encountering a soulmate is not as much in who he or she is, as it is in the why. These soulmates are linked to the aspects of our soul that have remained unmoved in time and need a transmutation.

This transmutation is never easy. More often than not, it will require the burning of toxic waste that we have been suppressing within ourselves, namely, old fears, old anxieties and old deceptions.

One of the things that I have noticed in these encounters, is that those who cry the most, also have the strongest layers of self-deception on top of them, blinding them to the truth about themselves. So many times I have heard the sentences:

— "You are the best person I have ever met";

And,

— "I can't stop crying, even if I don't want to see you again, and know that I will always miss you".

These sentences are sometimes spoken within the same conversation. And yes, this only occurs between soulmates. And yes, we have many coming to our life.

As we progress upwards and faster in our evolution, these soulmates will come more often into our realm. We will literally attract them as we shift the physical world around us and at the same time. But they also appear as part of those changes, to change us.

Without going too much outside this topic, I must tell you that speed is proportional to spiritual growth. So, the balance has to be acquired either by shifting reality or oneself. Nothing is unmoved once you start your ascension.

Those who think that meditation is a technique meant for more peace of mind are really deluded. For meditation is actually the technique that helps you in handling chaos. It wouldn't make sense to meditate if you could simply take time for a nap during the daytime or to smell the roses in a garden.

You see, one of the most interesting things about spiritual evolution is that it can't happen without breaking apart the negative karmic cycles that we have been living.

A very spiritual person is not more at peace. And, sadly, many of those who have met me, did the grave mistake of assuming that I am not spiritual because of how they perceive my life. They think that my life is too chaotic and out of control, and therefore that makes me not spiritual.

They wrongly assumed that, if I was indeed as wise as I appear to be in my books, I would be living a very peaceful life, would be happily married, with a family and a couple of children, and financially stable too, with a big team working for me. And I honestly really wish they were right. However, the simplest things never occur to those who are constantly creating chaos around them by transforming themselves faster than the rest of the world.

The Importance of Accepting Your Soulmate

I already knew, for a very long time, and almost since I was born and came to the realization of who I am, that my life would never be peaceful. The more I accepted my nature, the faster the world around me collapsed.

I eventually came to the conclusion that, if I wished to continue along this route and really make it work against the odds against me, I would have to let my entire world collapse and end in ashes. That was the price I was willing to pay and I paid it by accepting my nature. And so, it was with no surprise that I saw people entering and leaving my life really fast, that I saw people whom I trusted and helped in achieving their dreams, insulting me and pushing me away, people I helped both psychologically and financially, finding idiotic reasons to put me outside of their reality, and much, much more.

These experiences led me to accept that is not only the mechanics of the physical world that change rapidly to adjust to spiritual progress, but also the mechanics in the paradigms of others that, by not changing, have to reject our new self.

If humanity was truly synchronized with the world, you would probably not recognize the planet anymore. And yet, technology systematically gives us glimpses of such paradox, with wifi, lasers, electroencephalograms and more.

Such technology shows us an invisible world that affects us at all levels. And it is often the ignorance of how much this matters, that allows the development of technology that affects us negatively.

If the contrary was true, and the planet was synchronized with humanity, you would physically explode into many tiny pieces before you could evolve as a spiritual being.

Due to this gap, at the very last stage of this cycle, there is a complete sense of loneliness, or the awareness of such vacuum in the world. And it's a type of loneliness few would be able to endure.

This type of loneliness has a profound meaning. In simple terms, it means to be moving really fast in a world that moves very slowly, being in the world and not being part of the world at the same time, and meeting people who just don't understand us and feel the same separation we do, but that, despite this, don't want to create bridges to make things work, people who are too scared of what it implies to be connected to someone that can create significant changes in them and in their life.

Just months ago, a person I was starting a relationship with actually said to me:

— "It scares me that you know so much about me and my emotions, that you know my pains and worries and fears, and even thoughts, and that you know exactly how to make me happy. I'm sorry but I don't want to see you again".

How sad this is, for I was the person who would take her out of the darkness she was in. And that's why she fell in love with me.

She rejected her emotions to prioritize her logic — her mental patterns regarding how life and relationships should be.

I was also attracted to her but I already have too much experience to fall into these spiritual traps. I already knew that she would be too fragile to endure what was occurring between us. And so, it makes me laugh when such people consider themselves brave and strong, as was her case.

There is nothing of brave and strong in fearing falling in love with someone who can see the depths of your heart and soul. That's the greatest fear of all. And if you are afraid of your own path, you are a coward. And well, soulmates that find each other aren't cowards, but cowardice does drive them apart once they meet one another.

Why People Reject Their Soulmate

Unfortunately, most people tend to change in a downward spiral of resentment towards their past, and becoming more of themselves, thinking that their personality is natural, and not a construct of past experiences and beliefs, most of which restimulated by lives in other bodies.

For this reason, when someone encounters a soul from a past life, she also receives the opportunity to make a spiritual change within herself, as the one she loves, may also awaken rage in her, the same rage that triggers necessary transformations within the soul.

We can then ask ourselves if, knowingly or unknowingly, we would confront our negative emotions in order to embrace the opportunity to feel real love. Because the masses don't want to do this.

The masses are terribly afraid of anything that is negative and conflicting within themselves. And the obsession for comfort, outwards and inwards, drives many to what is called "positive thinking" but is actually an escape of reality.

When someone can't even confront the differences in personality types, that person has neglected the need to grow as an individual. And I'm not even addressing the topic from a spiritual viewpoint, but merely in what regards psychological maturity.

Actions that are motivated by basic instincts to attract pleasure and avoid pain, without considering higher goals, related to maturing and developing psychologically, emerge from very immature beings. And most humans these days present exactly this childlike attitude towards life.

Despite that and what they want their life to be, reality is not a candy store and the physical world is not a toy store. There are very deep consequences to the avoidance of spiritual growth, and no theory based on joyful thinking should ignore that, because no technique can avoid it anyway.

Now, we may wonder why do we fall in love with someone we met before and that brings back all that karma, why do we feel a mixture of passion and hatred towards the same person, and why do these relationships usually don't work. But could they ever work?

First of all, we must understand that we are never alone. During our existence on Earth, we encounter groups of people we met before. If you take into consideration that you have lived many lives on this planet, you only need to multiply the number of people from one lifetime in many more, to see the vast number of souls you should be meeting, and that, in most cases, you won't.

Furthermore, and as mentioned before, evolution presents a very interesting paradox, for when you are evolving at a faster speed, you also encounter more souls that you have met in previous lives. And you also develop faster cycles with them, which means that, from the outside, you will seem like a very social person without any real friends. Inside yourself, however, you will feel connected to many and understood by none.

That is exactly how a spiritual evolution feels like once discernment has been fully comprehended.

How to Recognize Behavior Patterns in a Soulmate

When you meet someone in particular, that you can recognize from a past life, you will find that such person is experiencing the same, as these encounters are more meaningful when compared to any other. This allows you to recognize patterns, in how they talk and act, rather than just in yourself. And those behavior patterns, upon revealing themselves to you, will also reveal the answers you need.

Most of those answers aren't necessary the ones we wish to know. And the more conscious you are, the more you need to be aware of this fact. For example, you may encounter someone that you were meant to find, someone that you want to love, and also realize that this person is already doomed to end her life shortly.

I have met several of those women too in my own life. And interestingly, they were the ones rejecting me, and not the opposite.

You see, the extension of their physical body has been shortened by their karma, and they met me, precisely to extend it. It is only natural that those who are more desperate for answers, find in me their soulmate. And it is also natural that their emotions towards me are stronger than what they feel for anyone else.

These women confirmed it in their own words:

— "I have never felt anything so strong for anyone else before."

Many times I have asked myself why do they push away their, quite literally, life source, and especially, after noticing this. And the answer is as obvious as the refusal: For the same reasons they have shorten their life.

They have damaged their consciousness with the wrong behaviors, the wrong beliefs, and a constant violation of their spiritual ethics. Many of these women have been evil to too many creatures, and not just other human beings, and have a pattern of abuse of others and themselves. They have embraced evilness as their nature.

Love, at this point, usually becomes something alien to them, strange even. The more they fall in love, the more they consider the option to cheat.

They can't feel comfort in a spiritual duality with someone who accepts them because they can't accept themselves either. And they can't repent and confront their own consciousness. The sense of goodness, of feeling good and being right, leaves them restless and with anxiety.

At one point, they are living a constant battle within their mind, against themselves. They are bored, they are angry and they are afraid, for no particular reason. And so, their mind has to construct its reasons to justify the emotions in the body. And that's how they destroy the opportunity to their own salvation.

When we truly love someone, we accept them, even when we know that they may not live a very long life. And so, it is strange when they are the ones rejecting us, but that's how they fulfill their own karma.

Another thing that such people don't realize, even when their karma is already manifesting itself in obvious ways, as was the case of a relationship I had with a 25yo who was already developing tumors in her body, is that miracles do happen when you embrace a soulmate.

The feeling of being in love with someone and completely trusting another person who can make us happy, beyond our own capacity to be happy on our own, changes the structure of our DNA, and that's exactly where the answer to our many diseases appear. In other words, love saves people.

How I Found a Great Soulmate

It was during the process of editing the previous chapter, inside a coffee shop in Poland, that I found my latest soulmate, and hopefully the last, because contrary to many others have I met before, we agree on everything, we admire each other, we easily laugh together, and we feel confident on the future of our relationship.

An encounter that should have lasted for a brief half an hour conversation during her lunch break at work, turned into an eight hours date, followed by passionate kissing, after she told her boss that she was sick and wouldn't go back to the office.

The reason why everything felt so natural on both sides, despite being incredibly fast for common standards, has to do with what this book explains, and can be resumed in three crucial elements:

- She does not have a history of alcohol or drug abuse, and is still too young to have been damaged by many traumatic relationships clouding her feelings and discernment;

- I was able to recognize every single sign of having found a soulmate when talking to her, which gave me a huge advantage when compared to other people. Because I felt very calm the whole time, in complete control of my thoughts, emotions and words, and never surprised by her questions or reactions to my answers. Without overwhelming her with anxiety or information, I was able to provide the exact answers she needed to hear to trust me and herself. And yet, I never told her that I was editing this book, or that I would add a chapter about our encounter, because it would simply scare her away, and create in her mind the idea that I was manipulating the encounter and her emotions;

- We have many needs that complement one another, and what could be perceived as neediness or selfishness, actually turned into a feeling of accomplishment on both sides. Because, by sharing them, we felt even more connected to each other. And the reason why I wasn't afraid to address this topic with her and expose myself so profoundly, is precisely because I had, at that point, already made my conclusion about the fact that she was a soulmate. In other words, I only had to look at myself to see where I am at this point in time, what my karma is right now, to know that she would have to reflect that. Once I told her that I was looking for someone to make me company, a life partner, and then joked about the fact that, if I had to leave the country, I would kidnap her and take her with me, she laughed and felt even more connected, because that's exactly what she wanted. She was looking for someone who would steal her from her own world and take her into more life experiences, although not with a foreigner would abandon her. She was not afraid to be a follower but under the right circumstances, and my answer covered much more sides of her personality than expected. In fact, she added that her previous boyfriend made her bored by never wanting to spend time with her, and that her current job is not very important to her.

The superficial details of our conversation were obviously very important to her, because as human beings, we are immersed in our perception of the physical world. But they were not important to me, because I knew she was merely manifesting worries that were irrelevant to our connection.

I had, nonetheless, to be careful in order not to touch her main fears.

- When she asked me why I had so many girlfriends, and if I was collecting a girlfriend in every country I visit, I had to humbly explain that I was unlucky in the previous relationships. I told her that my previous girlfriends, although very beautiful and committed, had serious mental problems, and I described exactly which ones by addressing specific behaviors I could not tolerate. And she felt identified with my descriptions, mainly because both of our latest partners were alcoholic;

• When she showed a concern about my job, I knew I could not lie, so I told her the truth, that I make a living as an author. And this is something that scares most women, as it doesn't seem like a reliable profession. But in her case, caused the opposite reaction. She answered that she always wanted to be with a smart and creative man;

• My religious beliefs also caused some apprehension in her, as I did not hide that I am a member of secretive groups with information I can't disclose. But I was able to dissolve those feelings by telling her that she did not have to believe in the same truths that I do. There was, nonetheless, one truth in which I needed her to believe, and so, I used it to change the topic. I asked her if she believes in God, and she answered yes. And with this answer, we gained a deeper trust in each other.

If I did not possess so much knowledge on this topic, I would have certainly failed that day. Because she is extremely attractive, and that would immediately cause anxiety in me and shake my self-confidence, leading me to say things to gain her approval that would most likely set us further apart.

How to Accept Your Karmic Challenges

Without the information provided here, I wouldn't be able to understand the meaning behind the questions of the girl in the previous story, and what she really wanted to know.

Every time we seemed to disagree on something, I could assume that we had nothing in common, or that our differences would cause future disagreements as well. But instead, I looked at every subject from a common perspective: the one that had united us that day.

Basically, without the knowledge of this book, I would fail. And I feel very blessed to have met her during the editing process, as, by having both events occurring simultaneously, I was able to keep the information fresh in my mind and apply it successfully.

The main karmic challenge was also very evident here, when she told me that she wants to become a professional DJ. Because that means I may spend many nights alone and worried while my future wife is partying.

The reason why this is the main karmic challenge is confirmed by a mirroring process, in which we understand that our partner reflects back at us what we have reflected on others, with resentment and disdain for their reflection on us.

Fundamentally, because I have resented too many women that have rejected me for having an independent and free lifestyle, I attracted a person seeking the same, so that I may also experience the same emotions that other women have felt towards me, and along this way learn to forgive them and myself, letting go of that past.

All the karmic challenges brought forward by our soulmate are meant to dissolve parts of our soul that are blocking our spiritual ascension, most of which are related to negative emotions and misunderstandings.

This fact becomes even more evident in situations that are outrageous for the vast majority, as in the case of narcissistic abuse.

Narcissists, or psychopaths and sociopaths in general, always seek to be in relationships with souls who are very empathic, compassionate and forgiving.

The contrast between an empath and a narcissist is so big, that one could question how does this even make any sense from a spiritual perspective. But because I have been in relationships with many narcissists and have sought these answers to help myself, I can guarantee you that, it was only when I found this fact, that everything made sense.

I was never able to avoid attracting narcissists or falling in love with them, despite the huge amount of knowledge I had accumulated. All my narcissists were a perfect match to my weaknesses and desires, and each one was more beautiful and sexual than the previous.

I eventually realized that knowledge would not set me free. And so, I looked at my soul, to understand what was keeping it unbalanced.

I realized that my narcissist soulmates made me question my social worth, my value as a human being, and that they were constantly picking on my insecurities and fears, namely, the fear of being alone or never married.

The answer was to actually accept the fears as possibilities, and work on the insecurities before addressing the possibilities.

The first thing I did, was to peacefully accept the possibility of never again having a healthy relationship. And so, every time I attracted a beautiful woman who seemed to have emotional or mental problems, I rejected her without any sense of guilt or resentment.

I then started doing more things alone, never questioning the need to do it with someone else. I started attending concerts and parties alone, and going to events on my own.

Whenever a woman insulted me and rejected me, I would not have any emotional reaction or blame her. I actually started accepting this without any remorse, and saying out loud: "That is why I am single".

THE 14 KARMIC LAWS OF LOVE

The more I accepted that I was consciously single and without guilt for being single, the easier life became. I was able to spend more time dedicated to my work, which brought me better results too.

Then, unexpectedly, God sent me this beautiful angel. This soulmate that I met in Poland has too many personality traits that I never thought I would find. She is very kind, selfless and focused in art and emotions, more than material gains or fame, and she has a wonderful smile that lightens a room and makes me feel lucky.

Now, as mentioned before, we have to take our soulmates with the challenges they bring us. And so, I had to simply not react negatively to her dream but support it, and take that challenge on myself, rather than blaming her for not wanting to be more committed.

It was a lot for one day, the first day we met. But that is also the reason why it made sense to move things so fast. I would not recommend doing the same without having sufficient information on the other person or on her reactions to yours.

How to Overwrite Your Fear Patterns

In today's world, is very easy to attract someone with lust, but very difficult to do the same with love. You can only attract someone with love by applying patterns that transcend your reality and will, and match the spiritual world. And that is why what I mentioned here only works when you find a soulmate.

Another important aspect to take into consideration is that, even if you can accomplish these miracles really fast, by using the information of the book, your mind will still be operating against you. Every day, my mind produces memories of my previous relationships, and fears of what might happen.

It is inevitable that our mind keeps comparing the present with the past, and making computations that, although meant to keep us safe from suffering again, can also keep us apart from its opposite.

These thoughts emerge from thought patterns formed by habit, or more precisely, fear patterns. And the only way to handle them, consists in controlling them with renewed beliefs.

You have to be able to set new beliefs for yourself in order to change your thinking patterns.

- One of the most important beliefs, is to know that miracles do happen;

- Another, is to believe that you deserve to be happy;

- And finally, a third and very important belief, is to have faith in your own spiritual work, and know that it is producing fruits in the form of new opportunities.

I have met many people that, after getting hurt too many times, become defensive, and by doing so, too sensitive and aggressive, which leads them to push away those that want to love them. They do this not only with potential lovers but also friends.

Many women have rejected me because I did not answer their messages fast enough, or because I did not kiss them on the first date, or because I refused to meet them in the exact day that they wanted. They made definitive decisions based on silly conclusions, due to thought patterns rooted in fear. But, because fear is the opposite of love, you push away love when making decisions based in fear.

These fear-based comparisons, although appearing superficially similar, are represented by different human beings. It would be like saying that everyone that dresses white thinks one way and everyone who dresses black thinks another way.

In another case, a friend who was dealing with narcissist abuse insulted me, because, one day I told her that I could not work while always talking about narcissists.

Sometimes, I simply couldn't talk to her about the topic to focus on my writing, which was unrelated. But, when I told her this, she exploded and out of nowhere started insulting everything she knew about me and my life.

That was a very stupid thing to do, especially after telling me that I was the only person helping her overcome her traumas. Because, if she had a therapist and was on medication, both were clearly not working as well as what I was giving her and for free.

Now that the friendship is over, she has sunk deeper into her abyss. And when you do that, and push away those who want your best, you also delay your healing.

Life is too short to be stupid. If you keep pushing away the people who love you due to thought patterns rooted in fear, you may only understand what love is when death knocks at your door. Healing, based on faith and hope, is necessary to eradicate fear and embrace the light that reflects in your heart through the many opportunities that appear in the reality you allow yourself to explore, and often beyond your expectations.

Why Faith in Your Karmic Path is So Important

It is said that thoughts change reality, but thoughts are nothing when compared to the power of surrendering oneself to something greater than us. That faith in the absolute, in an invisible pattern that governs our world, and our perceptions, can do anything, and very often does what we never considered possible.

To call it God, would be to confine its potential in the full spectrum of the many possibilities, because no human mind will ever be able to understand God when compared to all of His creations. It would be like asking an ant to explain the Universe. The ant barely understands its own physical world in all its extension.

The greatest leap one can give in that direction, consists in truly surrendering oneself, because only when you do that, do you give up on the idea that you are in control of your thoughts. You are not and you never were and you never will be.

Ultimately, thoughts don't change reality. Your self-perception of your thought do. And your self-perception transforms and is determined by your awareness. And your awareness never belonged to you.

It is like having eyes to see. You can feel blessed for having them, but you can't say you have eyes because you have chosen to have them, or that you can use them because you have chosen to do so. It's actually something beyond your control. And you can be as stupid as to blind yourself to prove something to others or to yourself. But you can't really make yourself see if the opposite is the case. And likewise, you can't make yourself see more on your own. You can only be ready for when the opportunity comes your way.

The same applies to your soulmates. You can be ready for when they appear and you can accept them but you can't find them on your own and you can't force them to accept you and love you. And that's probably one of the most traumatic experiences you will have in your evolution as a soul — to find a soulmate, love them with all your heart, and then suffer the pain of losing them. It will feel as if someone has cut off a part of your own body without any anestesia and the pain remais for months, even years.

This said, should we love again the same person as we loved before in another life? Or let him or her go and take everything as just another life experience?

In order to answer these questions, we must understand that there are many changes occurring in one lifetime and between reincarnations, meaning that the same individual will eventually interpret the same emotions differently and with different patterns, filtered through the experiences accumulated in each life.

We are never the same between lives, because of the vast amount of experiences that we accumulate through one lifetime and how they change our own sense of identity.

In fact, you will never grasp the sense of oneness of an individual, if you can't go through his personality. For most people, that's all they have. And so, it is with great confusion and anger, that many see me easily reach their spirit beyond their capacity to stop me. Because that's like moving through walls before their eyes.

You see, most people are so convinced that nobody can touch their spirit unless they allow it, that they actually think that they can project a certain personality unto others and have them there, under control, interacting with that personality they project, also known as the social mask.

That doesn't occur with me, because I ignore their personality and go straight to their core.

That scares them. Even causes horror in many. My own mother used to call me a monster because I could easily see her thoughts and fears. Her control was futile in the sense that she couldn't play with my mind as easily as she did with others around her. I awakened her deepest horrors. But in doing so, I was also the salvation she kept praying for and never had.

Sadly, she was too stupid to see it, and over time, and due to her blind trust on psychiatry, she just kept getting worse. Now in her sixties, she continually drives herself in mental cycles related to her past. She has ceased to evolve as a soul. And well, you will never find spiritual answers in those who deny the spirit, as it is the case of the experts in mental health, whom, despite their claims, are experts in nothing but denying responsibility for the very poor results they get.

The Importance of Your Decisions

When we love someone, we're not loving alone, and therefore, we don't encounter people from past lives for personal reasons only.

If two persons fall in love in one lifetime, but somehow can't fulfill their desires, they may certainly meet again and want to continue along that path, in order to close a spiritual cycle. This closure, naturally, emerges from the same reasons as to why we wish to reencounter those we lose in one lifetime — unexpected death, a treason leaving open wounds, deep feelings still attached to someone that for some reason we had to break apart with, and so on.

As we all know, from our own experiences right now, in this body, a large portion of those who entered our lives and departed, should have not done it in such way. We all wish many conflicts and misunderstandings had no occurred, we all, somehow, wish we could close old wounds, forgive, forget and love again, or at least be in good terms with many souls that entered our reality, instead of having resentment, hatred and sadness. And that's exactly why reincarnation exists. It closes those cycles by creating a balance between the visible and the invisible.

Obviously, such soulmates do have the capacity to choose what to do with every moment of their life. They can choose to love someone else instead too, and allow the purpose of the encounter with their soulmate to fadeaway and never repeat itself again.

They may even dream with the purpose they were supposed to accept, while neglecting the experience that brought that person to them. And how ironic, that people tend to dream the most about things they experienced before, in other lives, while assuming that it is part of a possible future.

Most of what people desire is a repetition of something that has already occurred, even though they often lose faith in themselves for not acting on that, for not accepting it, for being ignorant about the cycles of life and how experiences repeat themselves.

We always reencounter people we have met before, especially now that the spiritual cycles of the planet have been increasing in speed, and technology impels us towards faster connections.

The fact that it is much easier to cross the entire planet by airplane has certainly speedup our karmic cycles, making it much faster for anyone with the possibility to travel so much and freely to anywhere in the globe, to handle past life traumas and emotional blocks, and move upwards to a higher state of awareness.

Law 1: We reencounter those who are still emotionally connected to our spirit.

The Connection Between Desires and Reincarnations

Through our dreams and by using the power of our imagination, emerging from our subconscious conceptualizations of reality, we re-experience the past and the future, for in the past we find the experiences justifying our dreams, and in the future we have the potential reality of what we dream for waiting for us, and being attracted by the emotional vacuum formed by our past, although reshaped by our mind in the present.

If it wasn't for free will, one could design an entire life cycle for the spirit, and predict each one of his reincarnations and lessons. But whoever is gifted with premonition also quickly realizes something very interesting about humans beings, and that is that they tend to reject knowing what will happen, even when protecting themselves from self-harm.

Somehow, people intuitively know that they must fail in order to learn in the darkness, which isn't possible if a confrontation with trauma is delayed. And that is why having the ability to predict the future has not changed anything in my interactions with other people. For I may always know how my relationships end but I can't stop others from doing what they're destined to do.

Whenever I show people what I know about their future, they either want to discredit it to deny responsibly over a future event that has not yet occurred, or they basically delay the inevitable, up to a moment when unconsciousness, caused by fear, anger, anxiety, or the seduction of the wrong advice coming from someone else, makes them do what they were supposed to do from the start.

The mechanics of destiny are too complex to be predicted by anyone, for we are all connected in alchemic patterns that escape our awareness, and which guide absolutely everyone on planet Earth to betray their highest values and longest promises. Moreover, any stranger can shift the direction of whatsoever we believed to have under control.

In this sense, I must say to you that, our greatest enemies are our greatest allies too, for they force us to do what we otherwise wouldn't. Ironically, commonly out of jealousy, rivalry or simply motivated by evil, they push us in the right direction. And that, because both good and evil are under the same laws.

Could we then say that we receive betrayal more often from those we trusted the most when changing faster? Yes, we could.

The laws that command good and evil are present in three elements that we live by in a daily basis:

- The dream;
- The future potential manifested in a parallel reality;
- The past experiences related to our desires.

All these three elements manifest within one single image projected by our mind. That's why imagination is so powerful in controlling reality and leading it towards our desires.

By the force of habit, however, the large majority neglects their most powerful human skill.

Sadly, as I notice daily in the people around me, the majority is made too stupid and introverted inside their own beliefs, filtered by mass consciousness, in what regards what they think their world is, or should be, that they completely neglect everything that is presented to them by the quantum field — the spectrum of possibilities manifesting on the physical world.

The most important experiences of their life, pass by them unnoticed, and I can see why, as the facial expressions show me. People judge by what they see, and what they see is based on what they've experienced before, in their mind. And so, they go in circles of the same, reinforcing a mantra in their head, a paradigm, that is only real because they are the ones keeping it real.

That's what stupidity truly is — arrogance based on a self-imposed set of paradigms.

The Self-Deceptive Path of the Personality

People voluntarily put themselves in a jail of beliefs and lock themselves inside with a disdain for the spiritual world. In their egotistical view of themselves, they arrogantly believe to know everything, and indeed they do know, but it's an "everything" about very little — the little within themselves.

It's as if they kept reducing their own world of possibilities, while simultaneously rejecting the real world outside of them.

Then, when finally having to reach for that world outside of them, they do it through need, and in doing so, use the material world, not as fertile ground for opportunities, but rather a platform to satisfy emotional starvation and survival instincts. What they really seek, finds them, in the form of higher and deeper forms of deception, because such deceptions please their own egotistical wants and needs.

When such needs aren't met, they move on, thinking that this makes them more independent and self-sufficient and able, while in fact, with every single one of such behaviors, they close themselves furthermore inside a narcissistic mindset, in which the outside world is merely there to supply them, and not to interact with them and grow with them, change with them, and transform with their intervention.

The statistical evidence pointing at an alarming and fast growing trend in narcissistic personalities will never be fully understood before looking at the spiritual elements that cause it. Because you can't suppress love unless you first suppress the need for it. And the only way to do something so cruel is by deceiving people with the wrong values, values which they will embrace as their own, therefore causing their own self-destruction.

This is caused by creating a sense of need for the wrong things. Because the attitude of neediness, obviously, reduces the level of awareness in anyone, up to a state in which a dog can clearly see more than a normal human would.

In this sense, it is very interesting to notice that most people walk around like zombies, guided by subconscious instincts, and animals are the ones being more alert to the energies around them.

If animals were gifted with a higher intellect, they could certainly take advantage of the possibilities that humans ignore. Nonetheless, humans are gifted with a vast amount of psychological skills that lay dormant within them, and just because they're not put to use.

For us to say that humans apply only 5% of their brain capacity is a great overstatement, because in fact, they tend to use much less than that, even much less when compared to their ancestors, who were more aware of their spiritual faculties, as many ancient texts show us.

The majority of our brain is not, contrary to common belief, controlled by subconscious actions, but rather neglected. Surely, some of those areas come into activity when in need, but, because they aren't trained and used daily, when finally applied are typically handled in a very primitive way.

This is why the masses behave like idiots when confronted with diversity, art, deeper forms of empathy, love, and religion.

Most people are simply not evolved enough to understand these concepts, and applying them once a week on a Sunday congregation is also certainly far from enough for them to be able to consider themselves spiritual, much less religious.

To say that religion comes before spirituality would be like saying that dance comes before music.

Law 2: The spiritual mechanics guide us beyond our personal will.

How Karma Emerges From Emotional Connections

The most meaningful relationships I ever had occurred far much later than what I would expect, but I did meet the exact persons I was predicting I would encounter; and this occurred many times, leading me to ask myself the same question that everyone else does: Do we have one real soulmate or many? And if we have many, how is that possible?

In short, we do love and can love many people. The most common experience of this evidence comes in the form of a family. And yet, a family is not only circumscribed to the biological relations that some individuals have with us.

To think that our family is related to our body only, is a very primitive assumption of what life truly is, and not a spiritual way of seeing it either.

The relationship that we have with our family members, although must be prioritized for practical reasons, should never, in terms of compassion, surpass the affection we have for others around us. You should feel as connected to them as you do to any other human being. And you should be as willing to forgive a family member, as you are in forgiving anyone else.

Most people can only love their immediate family, because of the very low spiritual level they possess. They see reality foremost from a physical perspective, despite the claims of many that they themselves are spiritual.

In many cases, people can't even form an identity separated from the common traits found in the family, and these are usually the same which are commonly accepted outside their immediate circle of connections.

That is why, it is relatively easy to evaluate the spiritual level of anyone by the degree of importance such individual places on family values when compared to others.

When such values are compromised, the individual experiences a deep trauma from which he may never recover. Because the trauma uncovers the depth of the weakness of the soul, and such depth may have no ending at sight.

The more one does that, the less that person will consider his own values. But don't take my perspective for granted, as these things can easily be identified and studied in psychology too.

Almost all mental illnesses, or at least, the ones attributed to learned behavior and copied beliefs, can be traced back to childhood and the experience one has with his immediate family members.

Those experiences have the most significant impact on the personality, and some traumas can completely destroy a person's potential for healthy relationships throughout his entire life.

Now, even though families tend to operate as a tribe, reason why many people attribute their own survival to such connections, it's not always possible to establish positive emotional connections with our parents or relatives in general. And so, what can a family be, except a group which is able to evolve with you?

You see, having a family is a spiritual experience, but you can't force people into recognizing this, for not all will be able to see it.

Most people, including the ones who claim to believe in reincarnation, really don't understand anything about it and can't even begin to comprehend the fundamentals of this topic. For you never truly understand reincarnation unless you understand karma, which, inevitably, will show itself in your empathy towards the outside world.

You can't separate these areas when studying them.

The Relationship Between Reincarnation and the Ego

Many times, I tried to debate this topic with others, especially the ones who follow groups claiming to believe in reincarnation, and noticed that their ideas of reincarnation are typically grounded on fantasy.

In other words, they have mental constructs of whom they would like to be in a past life, but no idea whatsoever as to why they likely where or weren't such persons.

Naturally, people always want to use the topic of reincarnation to expand their ego furthermore, and put their low self-esteem to rest on some delusional idea of grandiose in another existence. But, you see, that's not the case with most souls, simply because we evolve with each life.

We don't and never go backwards. We can forget but we can't truly "un-know what we already know". Many of our acquired skills are easily remembered once exposed to the right environment and situations.

Allow me to explain this more clearly: You may not remember what you studied in primary school, but that doesn't mean that you can't multiply or divide. And you may not remember your best friend from childhood, when you were only 7yo, but that doesn't mean that, if you eventually encounter him somewhere, you won't feel a strange and strong emotional connection with that individual, who, nevertheless, will seem strange to you due to his appearance as an adult.

Have you ever had that feeling of *deja vu* with someone, in which you encounter a person that you are sure to have met before, and yet, can't seem to remember when or who that person is?

We all had such experiences. It's normal that we do. Because reincarnation is just a reality of our daily life and not merely a religious theory dissociated from it.

We can find the reason easily, as we then, after a short conversation, come to the conclusion of when we saw that person for the first time. But the really funny thing about such experiences, is when both of you are sure to have met before, and yet, both have no idea when, no explanation whatsoever about the possibilities, and on top of that, have completely different backgrounds, making it literally impossible to even have crossed the same paths in one lifetime. And, well, what about in another lifetime? Because, you see, the feeling is the same, except without a memory of it.

The Countries Where You Should Look for a Soulmate

I was not born in New York, and every single time I return to that city, I feel more at home than anywhere else in the world. I don't even need to try to talk to people, because they naturally want to talk to me, especially the women.

Most of my readers are from New York. And, when I encounter New Yorkers anywhere else in the world, they talk to me as if I was a local friend. In many cases, they tell me that they have never found anyone with whom they could talk so openly as with me and feel so connected. And so, I don't need a past-life regression to conclude I have been there before this lifetime.

This fact is proven by comparison with another, as I have always had the same reactions from the French, and recently did have a past-life regression in which I found that I had been French in another lifetime.

Now, with each life, we accumulate karma and leave behind karma too to be solved. Therefore, it is not always a good idea to return to where you have been murdered or murdered someone. For example, Poland and Lithuania are only divided by a border, as the two countries share the same history. And yet, in Poland I am loved, and in Lithuania I am hated.

The why can't be explained by the masses. But is easily uncovered in the minorities and the contradictions, i.e., the people who admire me in Lithuania and the people who hate me in Poland. For in the first case they are all followers of the ancient arts of war, and in the second, they are only old people with an outdated Soviet mentality.

I could be wrong here, but have to assume that I was most likely a Finnish Viking in one lifetime, pillaging Lithuanians of their resources and women, and a Polish Anarchist in another, fighting back the Soviets and the Nazis in the streets of Warsaw.

If you feel loved by the population of a country for no apparent reason, know that you have most likely done something good for its history. And the opposite is also true.

Now, there is one important aspect here that is worth mentioning, and it is related to soulmates. You are most likely to attract the right soulmates in countries where you have accumulated good karma, and bad soulmates in countries where you have accumulated bad karma. How the locals, in their vast majority, treat you, determines how heavy that karma is.

I find it hilarious when someone tells me that they feel good wherever they go in the world, as if that was a positive thing. Because when I look at their current life experience and karma, and compare it to how people behave around them, what I see is not positiveness but numbness.

In other words, they have never been anyone significant and have never done anything significant in the history of mankind either. Therefore, they have not accumulated any important skill for this lifetime, nor enemies. Their existence is just a complete numbness. It has no meaning. And that is exactly what they usually seek: meaning.

This is, quite frankly, a nice way to put it. They are literally stupid and unaware of it. Their consciousness represents a lower layer of development.

The Challenges of the Most Developed Souls

Every single time I found people in the upper layers of spiritual development, i.e., people who have accumulated many skills and knowledge from past lives, I saw the exact same problems in all of them:

- They struggle to fit in among others;

- They feel misunderstood;

- They are sometimes rejected aggressively for no apparent reason;

- They all have countries where they feel great and countries where they feel very bad.

If you feel any doubt about what I just said, compare and contrast within the same area of analysis.

For example, I was very welcomed in Finland, and always had good relations with most of the people I met from Iceland and Denmark. In other words, I tend to very easily make friends with those who descend from the Vikings.

If I look at Portugal, Spain, Britain and Holland, the same pattern occurs. I am always treated with rudeness and resentment in Portugal, but easily make friends with the Spanish and the Dutch. And, for reasons that the British I encounter can't explain, most of them distrust whatsoever I tell them. Why? Because this country was an ally of Portugal in wars against Holland, France and Spain.

As weird as it may seem, countries and cultures do accumulate karmic memories, and they manifest themselves when we expose ourselves to them. So, never assume that you can be in good terms with everyone, or successful anywhere you go, because we all have karmic lessons to learn, and they vary, depending on where we go.

When people travel to countries where they get murdered, that's a karmic payback right there.

Without going any further on this topic, we also assume that you naturally want to attract a soulmate that leads you to good experiences. And so, if you are smart, you will do that in a location where the energy works in your favor.

There are two types of memory and we typically operate only with one — the memory in our current brain. The memory of a past life is usually stored in our soul. Can be accessed by our brain, but is not in the brain; it's what is known as a spiritual memory. And yes, the spirit does record memories. Which ones? The same memories of the brain! Because the brain is basically a tool.

You are not own your brain, but a spiritual being using the brain. And that's why so many people are confused about this topic. They lack the fundamentals of how to understand reincarnation.

Once you understand that you are not your brain, you can see how the brain constantly filters the memories that are stored in your spirit. And your spirit carries them on, life after life, after life.

Why Do People Fear Believing in Past Lives?

We are not as terrified of believing in reincarnation as we are of all the things that it implies, once we open that door to our subconscious.

Those who fear the topic of reincarnation the most, are the same ones who fear the implications of karma as well, from this and past lives. And yes, you will see them quite often in religious congregations or working as a clinical psychologist, or psychiatrist, or even priest, because that's the best place, for someone who is terrified of what he has done to the world, to hide. You are usually betrayed the most by those you offer more trust because that's where their instinct tells them to hide.

The most evil people I ever encountered in my life, ended up becoming coaches, psychiatrists, nurses, and spokesmen of religious congregations, because nobody except me will ever see them for who they are. And that's why they hate me so much, for I am the one who can unveil their deception in public. In all of the cases I have encountered of religious congregations with such people, I noticed that they rather allow the demonic possessed to be amongst them, than someone like me, because I can reveal who the demonic possessed are and what kind of leaders they really have. And as both operate together, it is easy to target me as the undesired element. That's how the sheep — the majority, are led to the slaughterhouse; first through the fear of segregation, and then the fear of the devil himself.

Most people are not really running away from what it seems, but of what it comes after that, because to accept reincarnation, means to remember all the traumas you wish to forget, plus your responsibility over them.

This would be like having someone telling you of all the stupid things you did during childhood. You don't want that. You don't want to remember. Neither do you want to remember the many people who hurt you, or how you were hurt and how painful it felt. That's why you want to forget.

Forgetting is a blessing, to move on, and get more control over the present. However, just as much as your past in this lifetime still influences your views of the world and yourself, so does the memories of your past lives.

The fact that you forget doesn't mean that it's not all there, within you, stored in your subconscious mind, controlling you against your will, and affecting your thoughts and decisions.

As a matter of fact, most people in today's world are still operating under traumas of past lives and behaving like they are in the XVII century or far before that in time.

It did not surprise me, for example, when I met a Maltese girl in Spain, who was addicted to sadomasochism and attending shows where she was whipped in public and had candles burned in her body, as much as I was not surprised that she was able to do tarot readings, and spells, and draw the attention of many people towards her meetings.

She was a witch, and was burned alive in a past life, and came back to Spain to re-experience such trauma.

I could tell you many more stories of people who keep on living their past. It is relatively easy to see who they were, once you connect all the elements they keep dramatizing, as if reliving the same persona again, because everything matches too well to be a coincidence.

As a matter of fact, people already and naturally do this with the traumas of their current existence.

Basically, the fear of the topic of reincarnation, is the fear of being overwhelmed with guilt and memories one wishes to forget.

Why Do We Allow Our Fears to Destroy Our Dreams?

Have you noticed that, whenever a woman is traumatized due to a bad relationship, she keeps attracting the same type of man, again and again? Or that, when men are bullied in their childhood, they grow up to become insecure adults, attracting bullies at work? And, isn't it convenient that, those who seek the most love outside of themselves, end up feeling unloved in their adulthood? Or that, the ones who have prioritized their loneliness in order to reach their goals faster, later in life struggle to have meaningful connections despite all the skills they acquired?

Karma is not only something that you study in what regards cycles between lives, but a compound of experiences and self-created cycles of repetitive encounters that must be observed from within one lifetime too.

It doesn't make sense for me to talk to someone about her past life, if she cannot comprehend her own current life.

Should I say to a former girlfriend that she was a prostitute in a past life? It would probably do her no good. It would merely destroy her self-esteem furthermore. And yet, that wasn't as relevant as the fact that she kept behaving like one in her current life, and was unable to commit to anyone, including me, the only man who ever shared a house with her and proposed marriage.

Should I then tell her that, unless she stops acting like a whore, she will repeat this existence as she did previously, in another body, acting like a whore? And why should I feel entitled to judge her?

The only thing I could do was try, and I mean really just try, to explain to her how behaving like a whore would inevitably destroy her current life and her self-esteem; and that, by repeating old instincts, she would reinforce the karmic lessons that she had brought with her from birth.

In other words, if before her karma led her to a very traumatic childhood, this time, the same karma, would basically shorten her existence on Earth.

Indeed, she will probably die of cancer before reaching 40yo or some other deadly disease. Her body is already showing such outcome, as she easily develops cysts and has a weak immune system, despite being only 25yo.

Does this mean that she must necessarily die? No, it doesn't. That's why she met me.

Her karma is not as relevant as the decisions she makes. Because we build karma with our decisions too. We are the ones who create our own karma, and the ones with the power to end it.

Now, the question is: how can a narcissistic whore end her karma?

The answer should be very obvious and simple: by loving someone!

However, her karma consists in finding what she can't recognize: Who must she love?

The answer is: Her soulmate! But how can she identify her soulmate?

Her soulmate is the one she loves and hates the most, among all the men she ever met. He is the one who makes her feel addicted and scared at the same time. He is the one that she will never forget, but is too afraid to compromise with, due to fear of abandonment. He is the one that doesn't match what she wants (her narcissistic delusions), but rather what she needs (love with self-respect).

Whenever someone has a very heavy karma to pay, she either loves the one that pushes all the buttons of her soul and demands commitment, or she dies from a deadly disease, spending the remaining years of her existence fearing exactly that.

Life gives you options but all options guide you to the same principles and laws. And, quite simply, the heavier your karma, the more you need a soulmate.

Good people, with a light karma, can love anyone. And that's very obvious too, isn't it? Those who have a pure heart, appear to be naive, because they are easily lovable and empathetic.

Why Do We Need to Confront Our Karmic Cycles?

Our karmic cycles always lead us to either a repetition of impulses and habits that must vanish with the experience of their outcomes, or to a confrontation with our fears and traumas.

Personally, I always feared a crowd of stupid people, and my friends, naturally, kept telling me: "Why the hell do you care so much about how stupid other people are? Why aren't you just happy to be smarter than them?" But I couldn't help it, and that's why I studied the topic of learning disabilities, and then became a teacher, and eventually started writing books on learning and intelligence. I did not even considered writing more than books on education and learning, because my main purpose was to spread education in the world.

I was obsessed with helping people in not being stupid anymore, while always being easily triggered by the ignorance in others.

Eventually, I had to realize that I couldn't force people to learn and understand my knowledge and read more, and be less stupid. I had to give up on this obsession of changing the world with education. Despite that, I still couldn't stop finding myself anxious whenever I had to face stupidity in a group of people; I would always get very angry and start insulting everyone.

I was doing the same as a lecturer, and transforming my classrooms into a battlefield, in which I would invite the students to an open debate and then crush all their arguments by myself.

This habit, motivated by a strong instinct, changed when I found that I had been murdered by a crowd of peasants during the French Revolution, i.e., a bunch of stupid villagers that couldn't understand that they were being manipulated into doing that, and that their misery wasn't my fault.

In that fatal day, even my own soldiers betrayed me, which led me, towards the rest of my spiritual life, and into this present life as well, to never forgive anyone who betrays my trust or associates himself, or herself, with those who smear gossips and attempt to destroy my reputation behind my back.

How could I not react so aggressively and anxiously in such situations? I died exactly from that.

I would rather end a relationship than remain associated with someone who was interested in gossiping. I could smell death when my reputation was under attack. And yet, I also had to acknowledge that there was nothing I could have done back then or even now. The vast majority of the masses will always be stupid dumb sheep.

Moreover, knowing that, did not change the fact that I still have pleasure in writing meaningful books beyond the topic of education. But, knowing that, did make me less anxious about educating the world, wanting to change the world, or being a teacher again. I started focusing more on myself and on what gives me pleasure doing. And certainly, my writing style also changed a lot after that. You can still sense plenty of anger in my words, and you can still notice that I am educating in the way I write, but my main goal now is clearer, and more related to the present, rather than the past.

I am now putting my attention on a much higher level of meaning — in elevating the state of consciousness of humanity — as that's where my past lives have led me to, and because that's also my spiritual purpose in this lifetime.

The Influence of Karma in Our Spiritual Purpose

Our spiritual purpose often manifests before our awareness about it. And so, it is only natural that it took me so long to realize it, as I was, as many others, dramatizing my past, and not living my present.

Seeing my beautiful pregnant wife of blond and curly hair being decapitated in front of me during the French Revolution made me look at love as a transitory experience. For we never know how long it lasts, although it certainly never lasts forever.

That acknowledgement, by affecting my self-love and self-esteem by default, made me also want to write more from the heart and less from my brain.

After my past life regressions, I felt much less the need of telling people what to do with their life, and started showing more what occurs within my heart, so that they can feel the same. And these are indeed words that come from my heart.

Knowing the events and traumas that shape our attitude in the present doesn't automatically change our personality or choices. It is only a remembering, and you are still in command of your own destiny.

I am personally still attracted to petite blond women with curly hair, for example, because they subconsciously remind me of my French wife, and as much as I feel a sense of attraction and familiarity mixed with fear whenever I encounter a beautiful french woman.

It is actually an interesting coincidence that my last soulmate is also a petite blond with curly hair.

It is worth mentioning as well, that this trauma was not only mine, but shared with other protagonists, and I have reencountered many of my workers from that time in the many countries where I have been.

Now, did I get less worried about stupidity in the world? Certainly not! But I also don't feel so responsible for it anymore.

You can't control what the masses choose to do with their fate, despite the outcome that they are attracting by making decisions that affect their own destiny.

The French certainly paid the price of their revolution, for France never prospered after that but instead went into a greater economic depression with its wars, and keeps on dealing with massive protests to this day.

The world never seems to learn from such experiences, and keeps on repeating them, in what we can witness as global karmic cycles.

As an example, we see that people may nowadays wonder why were the jews so persecuted during world war two, and ignored by the rest of the world, while they are, themselves, doing the exact same thing to the muslims, and couldn't care less about what happens to them at the hands of the Chinese, whom, to a great extent, are doing the exact same thing that the Soviets and the Nazis did in the past.

People want to believe that the horrors of the past are over, but they keep repeating, because humanity does not learn from its past, and never will, for as long as it continues to reject the karmic influence of past lives.

It might be hard to believe that many nazis may now be living in Israel, but it wouldn't be a surprise, when, for example, you look at what they are doing to the Palestinians.

Law 3: Karma operates in cycles that repeat themselves if unsolved.

Why Love Reappears in a New Life

In order to understand the topic of love from past lives, or simply common affairs, furthermore, imagine that you are the king of a nation, you are married, but at the same time, you are also always surrounded by your employees, whom are your daily companions. Some of them take care of the horses, others take care of the chickens, and others cook the daily meals for you and the rest of the noble family.

Now, amidst them, one of the maids falls deeply in love for the king — you. And this king may also have feelings for the maid, but he can't betray the crown or the country, and assume his emotions over his duties as a king.

Every single day, he has to watch this girl, and feel seduced by her daily presence, to the point of delirium.

There will naturally come a point in which he starts daydreaming about seeing her naked, making love to her, and even, out of that obsession, begin conjuring opportunities to make it happen far from the sight of others.

We can call it lust, instinctual sexual desire, but whatever it is, humans have always felt it over what attracts them. The large majority of the sexual encounters in the world have always been based on lust over love. And that is why, most love stories seem more like fantasized lust stories.

It is, however, interesting to notice that, when a woman cheats on her husband, that always appears in stories as an example of true love, but when a man does the same, he is made a villain.

Whatsoever is the case, as in many other stories about love, eventually, this king can't even fall asleep, thinking about her, desiring her, and that's when her starts getting out of control.

He then wants to make love to his queen more often, to erase the madness from his head, but the more sex he has with his queen, the more he lusts over that young beautiful maid of fair and delicate facial features. And so, because we attract what we imagine the most happening, the opportunity manifests itself, when, during one of his sleepless nights, the king is walking by himself near the walls of his castle, and finds his maid.

After a short exchange of words, he is unable to resit her and kisses her. His hands follow, touching that delicate body that he immensely desired for so long and lusted after during every meal served. And not being able to stop himself, he asks her to escort him to an empty room of the castle, where they make love.

The maid, even though attracted to the king, also dares not resist him. Let's not forget that it's a different time period, and this king literally owns her life and everything she has. And so, the encounter may have happened only once, or not more than a couple of times, but the king, although regretting it, can't also stop himself from wanting her in his life.

Meanwhile, he knows that he can't make this girl the new queen and replace the current one, which is linked by agreements between noble families. And yet, the poor maid desires that and dreams about it every single night.

The maid is too humble, poor and naive, to even dare to ask the king for the possibility of marriage. She would never have the courage to ask the king to quit his title or to abandon the queen. And she also knows that if she tried that, she would most likely end up murdered in private by the associates of the monarchic family, or stabbed by the queen, or worse, humiliated in a public execution.

Never would the clergy support that as well, and never could she ask the king to quit his throne and become a mere peasant like she was.

Therefore, this girl dreams every night about her love. She literally falls in love with her king and starts desiring his company every night, not knowing if he will or not come through the door of her room. But she waits, and brushes her hair carefully, and even tries new skin treatments on herself, because she wants to be as beautiful as possible for her king.

THE 14 KARMIC LAWS OF LOVE

The people around her notice that she is in love, but nobody suspects with whom. And at this point, the queen may notice that something is wrong, and even hear rumors about it.

On the other hand, the queen also knows that she will never lose the throne or title, and confronting the king about it could make her end up murdered. And so, she also dares not handle this situation directly.

In this historical period, cheating on a woman was a normal thing. Therefore, the queen partially resigns herself to the times customs.

Motivated by resentment and fears, the queen must come to a point in time, in which she needs to handle this situation by herself, especially, when she finds it going out of control, with the king visiting his concubine almost every night and not even caring anymore about spending the night with his queen.

That is when the queen decides to reorganize the affairs of the castle, and send this girl somewhere else, far from the sight of the king.

The king may still be able to see his lover, but not so regularly, and not anymore without passing by many other people, who would clearly see what is happening, and would start to turn the rumors into facts, ending up destroying the reputation of the king.

His credibility would be damaged, and they could even murder the girl he was in love with to stop all that and avoid massive implications on the crown, which could put the country at risk of war with other neighboring kingdoms, as they would sense instability and lack of support from the king's followers.

The king can't do anything to change this but will never forget his beloved. And the poor girl spends the rest of her life crying about these memories. She may eventually marry a peasant like her, to maintain her social image of a good woman to others, but forever keeps that king in her heart and forever loves him.

This love is now on a spiritual level. The two have formed a psychological and spiritual bond beyond their bodies. And because the cycle is not fulfilled and completed, they will certainly desire to meet again. And they will, now with new bodies, and coming from different backgrounds, different nations.

When this girl meets that king again, in a new life, he is not an important person anymore, but just some random guy she encounters in a party. This guy, on the other hand, will present very different personality traits.

Naturally, if you are born arrogant in a poor environment, thinking that you have authority over others while not having it, you will be in fights all the time, you will get beaten often, and your own sense of entitlement to a crown will be trashed to pieces.

This king will not be the same confident man he once was, but a man lacking in self-confidence, shaped by his experiences of a new and less glorious life. He will still have an aura of monarchy around him, and he will still talk to people like he is above them, but he will also be more humble and less entitled. And this contradiction between strength and humility, certainly makes him more intriguing, desirable and mysterious to this girl, who feels captivated by his attitude.

The experience awakens the same emotions of a past life, and that's how she quickly falls in love with him again.

She is still not aware that she's loving the same person. She thinks that she is loving this person for the first time. Above that, she also doesn't know why he doesn't match anyone she ever imagined to marry with or anyone she has ever been with before. He seems to break the whole cycle of her past and question everything that her friends assumed about her personality and choices in men.

With the same emotions from a past life, appear the same beliefs connected to such emotions and incarnation. The guy from our story seems to not want others in the group to see that he is attracted to her, even though there's no logical reason for that; and this new girl feels stupid and undeserving when next to him, as if she was just a dumb peasant, even though she has a college degree now, and such thoughts make no sense either. But even though their thoughts seem to logically set them apart, what they feel in their heart pulls them together.

Once they confess their love for each other, everyone else feels surprised, because during the entire time, they were both hiding it in public, and talking only to other people, even when sitting next to each other. In other words, they repeat the same patterns of the past, because those are the behavior patterns that match the same emotions, even when logic makes them question why they do what they do.

The same mindset also follows the two into their relationship, for this girl doesn't like to work in a company and rather be a housemaid (which ends up being something she feels in conflict with, as she feels good in being a housemaid to her boyfriend but at the same time cultural education and social values raised her to think that this is wrong); and the king, even though born in a poor family, wishes to rebuild his empire, by creating his own businesses and having others work for him in the house, which, in other words, means that he would be very happy if his girlfriend doesn't have a job and is always at home.

Up to this point, it seems that we are witnessing a very weird relationship growing very well, except that, both are now in a new historically period, and their mind is filled with new values and rules, the same ones that people around them keep using to question the validity of their relationship and call them crazy for being together.

As time goes by under these circumstances, she will be first one to fail, being trapped by the idea of "with independent women, career comes first" at her office; or the "you are too young to be married and you should enjoy your life more" from her friends; or the "go out with your friends by yourself and get drunk to have fun" by her relatives and even her own psychologist.

Soon after, these two start fighting, again and again, over all these issues, imposed and repeated by outsiders, most of which this girl has known for a long time.

At one point, they are both battling inside their heart and mind, between emotions and values, about what they want and what they can't accept, what they love and what they hate.

As these conflicts persist, trust between them deteriorates, and the relationship inevitably comes to an end.

She finds a new man, matching the image that her friends and relatives kept passing on her of what an ideal man is, and cheats, thinking that she is jumping from one relationship unto another, much better than the previous.

Her soulmate then leaves to a new country, and karma comes back to her, because she is abandoned by her new lover. And she realizes that she has just failed her karmic lesson.

What is also interesting about this story is that both lovers repeated the same drama of their past reincarnation by being separated by other people once again.

Law 4: We find our soulmate to love again and grow with the experience by putting our emotions ahead of our social values.

Why Relationships Between Soulmates Fail

Life has a way to teach us the most profound lessons in the most painful forms.

The girl that I described chapters ago, left my life. And to my surprise, in the exact same day that I was going to edit this chapter.

It took me at least two days, immersed in my thoughts, doing absolutely nothing the whole day, before I could confront this book again and continue.

After going back to the chapter, "How I Found a Great Soulmate" and honestly realizing that there was nothing in that description that I could alter, I decided to be fully honest with my readers, while also taking these lessons on myself.

Our disagreement started online and not in person. And I must admit, it was my fault. I started it. I could see that she tried to dissolve my anger, but I could not stop myself, and things escalated too fast.

To analyze this situation, we need to look at two aspects, being one the psychological and the other the spiritual, or karmic. Psychologically, I am still resentful by all the emotional abuses and betrayals that I received in my previous relationships, and so is she.

Many people believe that it takes time to heal, but that's an unwise approach to the topic. You don't need time, but solutions and experiences that change you. You don't learn and heal by laying down in bed. You do that by changing your life, by being active, and in this case, by finding and loving the right person. Those changes will change you, and that is how you really heal.

As a matter of fact, both me and her, share the same scars, because she also struggles to trust in a relationship. That, I would say, is a common karma issue to be solved together.

Whatsoever is the approach chosen, we never forget our past, our struggles and sufferings. And, naturally, we do not want to be with someone who does what was once done to us.

I can understand that this girl needed to ask me many questions about my past, in order to understand how loyal I am. She doesn't believe in loyal men anymore. And I did my best to prove my loyalty, by telling her that I wanted to spend more time with her, including the weekends. I explicitly told her that I want her in my life. And so, she was very happy, knowing that she had finally found a man committed to her.

We must understand, nonetheless, that, as mentioned before, life, and karma in particular, is always mirroring back at us what we fear or need and want. So the question is: Was she being as loyal and committed as she demanded me to be?

A mirroring question in this case would be: If she was not being what she wanted me to be, could I control myself while being emotionally involved, and not fail in applying the same rules that I am telling my readers to follow?

This was a very big challenge, because I was still working on this book during our first days together. And due to the constant analysis of this theory, I could not separate my author brain from my reality, in which I had to just and simply be a man.

Instead of communicating with her as Dan the boyfriend, I communicated as Dan the author. And that is why all the analysis that I could provide you on the conversation is unnecessary, as it is included in the words I passed unto her.

Instead of the desired effect, she felt trapped, confused, frustrated, and did what most women would do in the same situation, if confronted with their behaviors in such a way. She cut off all communication.

I had failed, because being a good author, means being a horrible lover. I do not forgive easily and I do not forget easily, because I am constantly writing about values, moral and ethics. To ignore all that in the outside world is like violating my own principles.

I cannot be who I am and not be this person at the same time. That, interferes with my mental health, and eventually corrupts my capacity to write, as well as my ability to channel information and better insights.

I felt trapped in this situation, as much as I was trapping her, and the emotions took control over both of us.

On the other hand, as you will see here, I was also right in my observations. The problem is that, in relationships, you need to be wrong first in order to be right later, if this makes any sense. You need to tolerate a lot, before the other person willingly confronts her own issues.

The karma between us came to the surface, because the more she demanded my commitment, and the more committed I was, the more I started to question her own commitment. She brought karma on herself by forcing me to confront my own.

If she did not wish this to happen, she should have been more careful with her own karma. But she wasn't. She does not know anything about karma. She doesn't understand that life is always mirroring back at us what we think and do.

The truth is that I felt the need to ask why she always took so long to reply my messages. I asked her if she was texting with other men, to which she answered, "Not right now." And I felt like she was taking advantage of my good will, so I continued:

— "What do you mean by 'not right now'? Are you still texting with other men who want to be with you?'"

She sensed a fight starting with that question and tried to stop it, by changing the topic to something funny. And I felt that she was running away from something that matters a lot to me, i.e., betrayal, and so I felt the need to continue, pushing it further.

What followed was, quite simply, a battle for truth, in which a common karma was revealed. A karma that brought us together and ended up setting us apart, despite everything else, namely, the fact that we felt very good in each other's company, shared the same values, the same goals and dreams, and both of us wanted to build a family together, despite how fast it all went on both sides.

Quite literally, we both wanted the same things. And we both allowed karma to destroy our dreams.

When Two Soulmates Have a Quarrel

The transcription of the conversation between me and my soulmate contains all the analysis that you need, because, frankly, this is exactly what scared her away.

Anastasia: — Many people told me that they want a serious relationship, but in reality it turned out that is the other way around, and that is why I don't believe in this anymore.

Dan: — How many people told you that?

Anastasia: — Every person says so, but often it turns out that it is far from it actually. But I didn't have many men. Many want only sex from me and say a lot of serious things.

Dan: — I agree with you that many people lie. But I need to ask you: How many non serious relationships have you had? Because the number also affects how you see yourself. You don't need to believe me. I don't need you to believe me. I just need to know if you want to be with me. The rest, you will see in time. I will never ask you to do anything that you don't want to do. Are you still texting with other men because you don't believe me?

Anastasia: — Texting with men means nothing, I always wanted only a serious relationship, but I had only one because it happened. I do not know you very well yet to write what I want or not. I need time to understand. But you like me.

Dan: — You did not answer my questions. Are you still talking to other men and trying to find better? And how many relationships that were not serious did you have?

I do not need you to trust me. You believe or you don't believe. I cannot force you to believe me.

Yes, I like you. But if you make a mistake and destroy my trust in you, I can stop liking you very fast. I was betrayed many times. I do not forgive that.

Anastasia: — What is your character, are you a quick-tempered person or calm?

Dan: — My character is the one you already saw. But you are worrying me. How many men did you have in your life?

Anastasia: — This is a stupid question. This is also something personal. But I had less than five.

Dan: — If I ask, is not a stupid question.

You asked me why I had so many girlfriends but you also had quite a lot of men for your age. And you told me that you are looking for something serious, but you are not being serious if you keep texting with other men.

The more partners a woman has, the more difficult it is for her to trust anyone. That is why I asked.

Never say that my questions are stupid. They are not stupid for me. If you want me to be serious and honest with you, you have to be serious and honest with me. This is not a game.

If you are still talking to other men, it means that you are not very sure about me. If you are not very sure, I will do the same and talk to other women too.

As I said, this is not a game for me. Maybe you think that you want a serious relationship but you don't behave like you do.

Yesterday, we spent the evening together, and I told you that I want to spend more time with you. I said that I want you in my life. And then you went on to talk to other men. Why? You think I am a clown?

If you are still talking to other men, it means that you don't care about me, and you don't care about what I say, and you don't really want to be with me. It also means you are not very serious. So, maybe next time we go out together, you should pay for your own food and drinks, to prove that you are serious.

I don't like to be used as if I am stupid. If you cannot apologize and change your behaviors, you will never find anyone serious.

THE 14 KARMIC LAWS OF LOVE

I don't like to complain and to babysit. If you want to be with me, you need to grow up and be a woman, and stop cheating by talking to other men.

You are losing the value I saw in you.

Maybe the world is full of idiots, but I can travel the whole planet until I find the woman I want. So tell me: are you this woman?

I told you that I don't like to waste my time. So you just need to tell me if I am wasting it or not. Because I would not spend time with you and kiss you, if I did not see any purpose in that.

If you want to go out with other men, and compare, you just need to tell me in advance.

Yesterday I sent you a long message telling you what I want. And you replied: 'I understand but I am tired to answer'. But you were not too tired to chat with other men.

Now you call me stupid for asking questions. I never called you stupid. And I answered all of your questions. But maybe I was wrong about you. Maybe you are the one who doesn't know what she wants.

Maybe you are not serious. Maybe you are just playing with me like I am a toy.

What do you want from me Anastasia?

Anastasia: — Trust that, for my age, I didn't have many men.

How many serious relationships did you have?

Yes, I was often deceived, so I'm always sure of what I see. And what I see from this conversation is that you speak like a capricious child who is trying to manipulate and judge by the framework of absolutism and his own stereotypes but is not ready to trust anyone.

Trust is a two-way road. If you are not ready to trust me, then you don't need a serious relationship and pleasant pastime.

Serious relationships are always a risk, but you are not ready to take risks and you only need the result. So why should I be your girlfriend if you are not ready to become my man?

Dan: — How can I trust you, if you don't know what you want, and you keep talking to other men? Are you going out with different men too?

I don't want to be cheated. But I think you can answer your own question: Are you ready to be my girlfriend?

Anastasia: — We should be as friends but a friends' relationship needs trust, and you are not ready.

Dan: — You keep saying that I am not ready but you are the one texting with other men after spending time with me. You are the one who has men always texting.

You say that they are just friends. I don't know that.

You can't ask for trust. Trust is something that you deserve with behaviors.

You said that I am afraid to be your boyfriend but you are the one who can't even say that you want to be my girlfriend. And you say that I am arrogant and have stereotypes but you are the one who keeps calling me a liar, even if I always told you the truth and you lied to me. So who is manipulating? You!

I am not ready? I told you that I wanted you in my life, and I told you that I wanted to spend more time with you. I also told you where I am renting my apartment next month and I told you that I want you to spend the weekends with me.

What did you do to prove that you want to be with me? How can you say that I am not ready? You are the one who is not ready!

You should apologize for your behaviors and mistakes but you can't to that. But you say that I only want the result. What is this that you are doing? You are the one who wants the results but makes no efforts.

THE 14 KARMIC LAWS OF LOVE

Everything that you said about me is wrong. And that is ok. But it tells me a lot about you.

You said that a relationship has two ways. I did my part since the first day. If you think it is two ways, and you don't have to respect me or trust me, then we can split the bills in two, and you can delete the contacts of other men who want to be with you, and you can also put on your social media that you are in a relationship with me for everyone to know and for the men who want sex with you to disappear.

Can you do that? You can't! But I don't care if my friends know that I am in a relationship with you. That is why I hold your hand in the street.

You are the one who is afraid! So don't insult me!

I don't know if you are dating different men when you are not with me. I don't know what you write to other men when you say that you are too busy to talk to me. I don't know if you are kissing other men too. How can I trust you?

You said that all men cheat. Did I cheat on you? No! Did you cheat on me? I don't know! That's the problem! Because maybe you think it is not cheating if in your head we are not in a serious relationship. So what do you want from me?

I make a living as an author of books on psychology and spirituality, so never assume that I don't know more than most people, because when you do that, you lose an opportunity to learn. And you need to learn many things.

One thing you need to learn is to love. You want a relationship but you are afraid to love.

I asked if you are dating different men at the same time. You gave me no answer.

I asked if you are kissing other men too. You also did not answer.

I asked if you are flirting with other men, and you said, 'not today'.

Nevertheless, you tell me that I am the one who is not ready? Ready for what?

I don't like to spend money on women who are not mine.

Just now, I asked many questions and you could not answer any of them. But feel free to put on social media that you are in a relationship with me and tag me as your boyfriend, if you have the courage for that.

I don't think you can do that. Because you are afraid to lose the attention of other men. But you say that I am afraid to take risks? This has nothing to do with risk. I am not stupid. If you are spending time with me and then talking to other men who want to be with you, that is cheating.

You need to look at your behaviors, if you really want a serious relationship. And if you really want a relationship with me, you should answer all my questions and answer with the truth. Just like I did with you. Can you see the difference?

You said that you did not have many men, but all that anger inside of you, and distrust in me, and fear of commitment, proves that you did have more men than you should.

If you want a serious relationship, you need to start seeing the differences in men. And I don't think you can see the difference between me and other men.

If you cannot see the differences between me and another men, why should I be with you? To be insulted? Why should I tell you that I like you, if you don't like me?

Maybe you just like the attention, and that is a problem.

I wrote many things but it feels like I am talking alone.

Anastasia: — I'm sorry for insulting you, but you disappointed me.

Dan: — I disappointed you? Or you disappointed me?

You are flirting with other men and talking with other men after spending the evening with me, and I disappointed you? Are you making fun of me? I wrote all these messages and you answer that I disappointed you?

THE 14 KARMIC LAWS OF LOVE

You know what Anastasia, you are not who I thought, and I feel very sad.

You talk a lot about manipulation but you are the one who uses it in the conversations. You are not honest.

Maybe I disappointed you because I am not as stupid as you wanted me to be, and I don't tolerate cheating behaviors and lack of respect and insults. This is what you are doing.

You are playing games. You are not serious. That is why you cannot find a serious man.

You found one. You found me. But you are not serious, as a woman.

How can you say that I disappointed you, when you are cheating on me? Are you insane?

You are seeing different men but you tell me that I am the one who is afraid of serious relationships. Is this a joke?

I asked you if you want to be my girlfriend. What is your answer? Nothing!

I asked if you have the courage to put on social media that you are in a relationship with me? What is your answer? Nothing!

Anastasia, if you want a serious relationship, behave like you want one. I already told you how. It's not difficult.

Put your ego in the trashcan and send your pride out of the house, and do what I tell you, and you can have a serious relationship with me.

I am giving you another change because I like you.

I thought that you are shy but you are not shy. You are just confused because you are keeping many men at the same time. You need to choose one.

If you want me, you know what you must do. Don't ask me to trust a cheater.

If you talk with other men who are interested in you, you are cheating on me. If you think that we kiss and hold hands outside but that is not a relationship, just a friendship, then maybe you are not ready for a serious relationship yourself. So what do you really want from me?

You will be ready for a serious relationship when you can choose one man and ignore others. You will be ready for a serious relationship with me when you learn to respect me.

I almost never kiss women in the first date. I kissed you because I wanted you. But you keep talking to other men. And you say I disappointed you?

There is too much hate inside of you. I don't know if you can love a man. And I need a woman who can love.

You want me to be your man but I don't know if you can be my woman.

It's very easy to find a bad woman. A good woman is difficult. But I don't want a cheater.

Put on social media that you are in a relationship with me, and erase the contacts of men who flirt with you, and then I will believe you.

(Anastasia never replied anymore. She simply blocked all contacts between us. And I tried to call her several times in the following day in order to talk to her but she refused to pick any calls).

Why Karma Destroys Relationships

If everything seems to match so perfectly well between soulmates, why do such relationships often end?

Basically, as demonstrated before, with a real story, it happens due to lack of sufficient consciousness on what has occurred before, or as to why it repeats itself again.

You see, we are so obsessed with what others think, what they want or not, how they value us or not, i.e., social validation, reputation and acceptance, that we end up depending on the opinions of friends and relatives when making important decisions.

Other times, we are so immersed in our emotions, that we fail in applying what we already know, as it was with my case.

In doing so, we literally permit ourselves to either reinforce or destroy what we already have, based on how we feel or what others expect of us.

If you allow yourself to be guided by what others see and say, or the past, then you will certainly lose your soulmate, for a soulmate comes not from the current reality but a much older emotional link, one that finds answers in your own eternal spirit. And because of that, becoming part of one of the most important moments of our entire life — the day we find our eternal self through love.

As most people don't believe or understand what reincarnation really is, or how it expresses itself in love, you can't expect them to see, realize or even respect the connections you make based on such awareness.

This applies to your soulmate as much as it applies for the people surrounding her, because that person will most likely attract opinions that reinforce her fears, causing her to question the validity of the positive emotions and the value of the encounter.

I am sure that in my stories, this is what happened, which makes it somehow ironic, as they usually say that I am the one who is not ready.

I must state that is not very easy to be ready alone, i.e., commit before our partner does the same. The risk is too high. Besides, it is valid on both sides. Because why should I commit with someone who is not committed? Why shouldn't I also flirt and talk with different women before giving myself to one?

You see, this is exactly what the problem is, people feel entitled to things that they are not entitled to. And that's disrespect. And you don't get love without respect.

Karma comes back to bite those people in the ass, because I certainly doubt that the women in my stories will ever find real love in their life. I don't know anyone that did by behaving like that.

From my standpoint, I did try to analyze myself, as to why I attracted this karma on me. And the only thing I can see, is that I need to stop taking responsibility for the mistakes of others, and not blame myself for the consequences of my natural distrust.

In other words, I need to respect myself more. And isn't this interesting? Because during the whole conversation with my latest soulmate, I was demanding her to respect me, in order to be in a relationship with me. I was mirroring my own karma.

She could not respect me, because she did not see self-respect in me either. And so, she did what felt natural to her, which meant to ignore me.

On the other hand, it is interesting to remember that my first thought, when she acknowledged that she was keeping in contact with other men, was to do what she did to me, i.e., block all contacts with her. If I had done that, I would have proven to have self-respect. Maybe even force it on her, and in doing so, keep her.

I will never know for sure. However, what did not change here, was the fact that I was confronted with my own karmic lessons, meaning that, one way or another, this would have to happen.

Both of us lost here. But I did not lose as much as she did. Because with this knowledge, I can self-analyze, improve and learn, and repeat the process again, with someone else.

She, on the other hand, will continue to grow resentful, because, as you saw from the conversation, she is incapable of self-analysis, and this is a strong sign of psychopathy. Psychopaths don't become better with time, but worse.

She believes that she is trying to find trust and commitment, while what she is actually trying to find is her true self.

She has nothing but a social mask. And the distrust she has on the world is a reflection of her own low self-esteem. With every failure, that fact will become more self-evident.

Why We Allow The Past to Repeat Itself

Quite often, we allow the perception of others to determine our fate. And we may think that we are dealing with a soulmate, when in fact we are dealing with her karma, the karma of the friends and family, and her emotional reactions to our emotional reactions.

In resume, we deal with much more than the interaction between two people who should simply love each other and trust each other.

We think that we are confronting the behaviors of others, while in fact we are confronting our own beliefs, based on previous relationships. And how can we create a new future, when we keep repeating the past? How can we trust, if we keep distrusting? And how can we demand trust, when we behave like someone who is not trustworthy?

The only thing a person can justify with her own fears, is the need to keep them. That is why we allow others to damage our self-confidence and question our choices.

This, however, only occurs because it is related to social appearances:

- "He is too ugly for you";
- "His job is not reliable for raising a family";
- "He is too old for you";
- "You two don't look good together";
- "You two don't match".

On and on, people will endlessly put traps in the relationships of others and attempt to destroy them, quite simply, because they don't fulfill their own expectations.

In other words, they judge your relationships based on what they themselves want and expect.

That's how much the selfishness of others poisons our relationships, if we do allow that to happen. But what right do others have to tell you how to live your life? As much as you give them.

If you can't make your own choices and instead follow others' opinions, they end up owning your destiny. And how sad it is, when a woman allows her female friends to rewrite the whole story of her life. But that's exactly what happens with most women.

I have lost many friends too because of that, because they truly believed they had the right to tell me what to do with my own life.

Most people get furious when you don't care about what they want, because they see friendships as a form of control over a person. Your decisions seem to affect their own self-worth and self-value.

In fact, many relationships are also seen as some form of exchange of control between two individuals. And this is what makes both friendships and relationships so sick these days. And yet, most people then say these things are normal. But having them being common doesn't make them normal.

We must, nevertheless, distinguish control from mutual respect, for it is not the same thing. When someone cares about the relationship, that person will want to keep it safe, avoid the possibility of being cheated, and invest in a common future.

A selfish person, will disregard that, and consider a relationship to be two people sharing a house while living completely different lives. That may sound ideal, but is not the reason why people get married, or at least shouldn't be.

The egotistical wants of each person, don't make any sense in a marriage. Because a marriage has more to do with compromise than with sharing different lives together. And until the world population understands this, marriage will always have a high probability of failure.

It is a mystery as why people still want to get married despite knowing that it will most likely fail, unless they have the delusional hope that they can beat the odds using the same values and beliefs as anyone else.

THE 14 KARMIC LAWS OF LOVE

Law 5: If we allow others to influence our decisions, we may pay karma until the end of our life.

Why Soulmates are Usually Different Individuals

The previous topic brings me to another very important one, related to independence, which is highly debated, but not properly understood by almost anyone I encounter.

It's actually interesting to see how so many people talk about things they don't really understand anything about, while full of confidence and arrogance in their words. Some even go on TV to spread these dumb ideas furthermore, because the imbecility of their head isn't enough for the small circle of damage they create, and they need to expand.

You known, it's like when you leave a baby pooping alone and suddenly you come back to the bathroom and see the walls full of poop; most people never grow past that stage; they keep on putting their hands full of poop everywhere, in the walls of the life of their friends, relatives, and even strangers.

I can't think of a better analogy than babies, because the only similar one is found in dogs, that need to pee everywhere to mark their territory. It is the idea of "if I pee on the life of my friend, he then belongs to me."

That certainly explains why, when I refuse to let people "poop" or "pee" on my life, they suddenly get very angry and frustrated, and move on to insult me, and then disappear forever from sight. They have a childlike and very immature attitude to life.

Women who fall trap to the advice of friends and social ideologies, quite often, make poor choices in their relationships as well, allowing the right man to vanish from their life. And they then move on to their 40s as unattractive single mothers. And I'm sorry if it's painful to know this, but that's karma. You never get as much as what you give.

We may have different types of karma to experience, but ultimately, some things, related to maturity, should be obvious, and quite often, are not. Most people lack a basic understanding on how to behave in social interactions.

As women are much more easily socially influenced by political propaganda and cultural values, or ideas that conflict with their spirituality, they also tend to be the ones paying the heaviest toll of karma. Their anger at the world, frustration, unhappiness, and overall misery, when realizing much later in life that they have been fooled into the wrong beliefs, is how they exteriorize such karma.

Karma is basically the law of cause and effect, while our emotions emerging from such cycle, are a manifestation of consciousness, when irresponsibility and lack of independent decisions, lack of moral and disdain for spiritual values, cause us to increase our karmic debt.

Once you lose your attractiveness, that debt is certainly much more difficult to pay back. But that is also how the laws of spirituality force you to use your heart much more than you ever did before.

The Mental Battle Between Soul and Society

Contrary to popular belief, a person who is truly independent is not one who does whatever she wants, and leaves the husband at home while she parties with her female friends, but both women and men don't seem to get this right.

Let me explain it more clearly: A truly independent human being, is one who is not afraid to lose his friends and the support of his family in order to prioritize his goals, and those goals may very well be loving one person only.

You simply cannot sell your spiritual path to the approval of others, or you end up increasing the karma you already have, rather that solving it and attracting a more fulfilling lifestyle.

If you keep on loving with your brain — and that's what matching your boyfriend with the expectations of others on you really is — you don't deserve any love, spiritual or not, or any relationship whatsoever, but merely a superficial arrangement.

Quite ironically, this is what most people waste their youth doing. They devalue their spiritual worth and increase their karmic debt, by having sex with as many strangers as possible, while setting their emotions aside, in order to find a better compatibility.

That certainly makes them less human and less capable of identifying a soulmate, or even make independent choices in life.

Those who follow such practices, then keep on maintaining the same mindset when wanting someone who matches a bunch of superficial expectations, regarding appearance, social status and even wealth. Emotions are completely discarded as secondary.

You can surely overcome all this social insanity with ethics and a deeper understanding of your spiritual nature. But where will you learn that? In religion?

I have never found one religious group that truly reaches this level, despite their claims. And even if you do reach this stage of consciousness, you will still have to deal with the level of consciousness of your partner and society as a whole. If your partner doesn't understand the need to commit, both mentally and physically, then you will end up paying the price for his or her karma.

If your partner can't go beyond what others think of him, and keeps nagging about what you should be or not, while making wild claims that have not even a resemblance with your true character and goals in life, you need to let him or her go. And yes, even if it's your soulmate. Let him or her waste another reincarnation on stupidity and move on with your own life.

I often feel guilty about my interactions with soulmates that just can't see what they are doing wrong. And then I look at myself, and realize I am suffering because of them, which I don't have to.

I wasted three years of my life in Lithuania because of a soulmate that was just going nowhere, and keeping me in circles of abuse, until I moved to Poland, where I found another, too needy to realize she is unable to commit to anyone.

But what else can I say? At least, I am moving forwards in life and learning my lessons. I do my best to live by what I write, and that's how I keep my mental health safe.

Don't allow your spiritual evolution to be delayed by an idiot. Your life is worth more than that. And the same applies to your friends. We don't all evolve at the same speed, and you should not be apologetic when wanting to be happy, because life is too short for long term mistakes.

The Transition Between Our Emotional Dilemmas

When I say that people bring forth emotions from their past lives, I am also including the negative ones and not only positive.

How do you think, for example, that a poor village girl would feel after being abandoned? Insecure, betrayed and abandoned. These same negative emotions are then reinforced by every single man that does the same to her in her next life.

Promiscuity, not only brings back painful memories associated with traumas from previous reincarnations, but also reinforces the same fears. By the time this girl meets her soulmate, her brain will be so screwed, that she won't be able to accept him in any healthy way.

These same negative feelings will emerge even more strongly as she develops the same positive nurturing feelings she had before. And this, because often, people can't distinguish present experiences from past life experiences, living in a kind of hypnosis to a certain degree.

The rapid exchange of connections that most people have these days, would require a very high level of spiritual and mental maturity that they simply don't have.

In fact, when you combine such level of maturity with the decadent state of the world right now, you should be expecting strong and long lasting relationships, even more when comparing to what our grandparents experienced. But you see the opposite. Why? Because the gap between the emotional and physical needs of the world has increased when compared to the level of maturity and intelligence of the population, which has vastly decreased.

The world has become more chaotic and unpredictable while people have become more stupid and selfish, and that's not a good combination.

As people tend to repeat the same emotions for many centuries over the same experiences, the girl of our medieval story will most likely feel fear and insecurity once in a stable relationship with anyone and for the rest of her life.

She will move on to the next life as a total failure, without any memories of the past life, but with a higher level of insecurity in what regards relationships; and it is not difficult to predict her next reincarnation, as easily as I can predict her future in this lifetime.

As a matter of fact, I was right in predicting the future of everyone I met, because at one point, these karmic rules become so obvious, due to the repetition of the same cycles, that no matter how much someone tries to escape them, they just keep on reinforcing themselves more in the same cycle, like a rope that tightens harder the more you struggle to escape it.

If someone wishes to escape karma, the only way out is within, i.e., through moral actions and a lifestyle guided by the heart, and in which free will is always following along this path.

Those who attempt to escape it, become predictable and not in a good way.

The girl of this story will never have a normal relationship for the rest of her life, she will try and others will make her believe that such is possible, and even help her, but she will always fail at one point. And she will fail because of how her heart betrays her every single time that she tries to love a man based on physical attraction or wealth, and especially, after rejecting one or many soulmates that she was supposed to treasure and love.

She will move on to her 40s as just another woman who lost her youth and attractiveness to foolishness and promiscuity. And as this will build up more frustration and sexual anxiety, she will move on to the next life with the same issues under a higher emotional pressure, i.e., more profound fears and more anxieties. And these emotions will manifest again and as soon as she tries to have a normal relationship.

This said, and because mental health and decisions can always be attributed to past life experiences and traumas, we can clearly predict that this woman will become a sexual worker in her next life, most likely a porn star or a prostitute, or both, or something else related.

Although it is not our right to judge, we do have the right to observe. And it's not uncommon to observe many sex workers who, despite repenting their past, would have done exactly the same, if they could go back in time.

These situations are likely to repeat themselves in the future. The normalization and acceptance of pornography, prostitution, sadomasochism and sexual perversions in our society, does not tell us that we are evolving and becoming more tolerant, but that we are degrading.

That normalization is merely the acceptance of a mental disease, so widespread that it has now become too common to be ignored or rejected.

Normalizing prostitution and perversion doesn't make one more evolved than others, as much as normalizing murder, bestiality and pedophilia doesn't.

Even though many would claim that these things can't be compared, I can assure you that they can, because these are the signs of a world in its last days.

Bestiality is becoming the norm in many erotica book titles, pedophilia is becoming more seductive than prostitution to many politicians and priests, and murder is in nearly all the most popular movies.

People crave blood and sexual perversions, and they are having them. And this will certainly lead to an increase of the karmic debt at a global scale, which at one point can't be repaid anymore on this planet, except through a mass extinction of the human race.

Another side of this is narcissism, because narcissistic attitudes to life blind one to the capacity to self-analyze, reflect on his behaviors, feel empathy for others, and change.

Law 6: You can only solve your karma with moral behavior and ethical decisions inspired by your heart.

Why Do We Repeat The Same Stories

When we can't remember our past lives, and don't even believe in reincarnation, the drama of our existence assumes a greater dimension and its most profound impact too.

Those who don't believe in reincarnation and don't understand what reincarnation is, are the ones who suffer the most with their karma, and especially, in their relationships, due precisely to such lack of awareness.

It is with no surprise that people now are so afraid to fall in love, and rather have sex with strangers without taking things seriously. As the soul gets older and accumulates more emotional trauma, love becomes a very serious topic, and ignorance, obviously, makes us fear our emotions even more.

If we are not aware of how our emotions affect us, we can lose the chance of re-experiencing a past love again. And yet, that doesn't mean that we won't encounter another soulmate after losing the previous.

We can always love again and again. But every soulmate awakens different experiences in us, because of the soul's memories within us, and that's why love feels so different with the different people we bring to our life.

That is also the beauty of love — the memories it awakens within us.

Most of us, relive those memories in the form of dramas. But with wisdom and ethics, they can be re-experienced with joy and appreciation. This is what this book proposes you and that's why it was written, so that you may learn how to love your soulmate, even when he or she is too dumb to know how to love you back, or at least, respect you.

Trust, as mentioned before, is not something anyone must be obliged to give, unless earned. A person cannot demand trust without being trustworthy. That's called emotional abuse.

The concept of soulmate is attributed, basically, to someone whom you've loved before. That's why the emotions remain strong between lives.

We always have different emotions with different people, because we have met them before in different circumstances, different historical periods. But the stronger the emotions are, the more important the role they had in your life. And consequently, the more important the karmic lessons will be.

Nobody can help us as much as our soulmates, although we always expect such lessons to be more beautiful and less dramatic.

The drama only occurs because people are unaware of the reasons bringing them together, and awakening profound feelings in them.

Surely, superficial relationships are much easier, and that's why people tend to prefer them, because, you see, if the emotions are not so strong, and you are both more stuck to mental compatibility, similar intelligence level and so on, it's much easier to make decisions together and reach a consensus, most of the times; the relationship is more stable and more peaceful and more productive too.

Such couples tend to be better at raising children, managing their finances and reaching their goals. And yet, how paradoxically interesting it is, that many of them divorce due to lack of passion, a boring sex life, and lack of interest in each other.

Obviously, difficult relationships can evolve into the same peaceful and joyful ones that others have, but that requires maturity and, commonly, people are either too mature and not spiritually aware, or they are very spiritual but immature.

If you can match both elements, then you get the benefits of two worlds — the logical brain from this lifetime, and the spiritual desire and passion from the previous, again, multiplied by each sexual encounter. Because, you see, it's only with a soulmate, that the more intimacy you have, the more you want to have, as at one point, you don't even look at intimacy as physical anymore, but a spiritual ritual between two beings enjoying each other's presence.

Sex literally becomes a celebration of joy in these situations, and for this reason it's also far much more enjoyable between soulmates.

The Importance of Sex Between Soulmates

People who have horrible sex lives always laugh when I tell them, as they can't believe it, that physical sex is far much more inferior to spiritual sex. And there is no way to make them understand this, except through sex itself, because it's a very organic and personal experience.

When you connect to a person on a spiritual level, you reach a stage of experience that few even know to exist. And that's such a high level when compared to physical sex with a random person, that it can be very addictive too.

This is the type of drug that people should be seeking the most: Addiction to spiritual sex with a soulmate. Nothing is more elevated than that.

It also makes the concept of orgasm obsolete. But obviously, one needs to experience it, to understand, by experience, why it is an experience above orgasm, which offers a physical climax only.

Now, if most women can't even reach physical climax with their partners, imagine what would happen if you introduced them to the concept of spiritual climax? That's simply too much for most souls on the planet today to conceptualize.

Humans on Earth are not evolved enough to be able to understand this or even handle it when they experience it.

My girlfriends would typically find themselves exhausted and extremely mentally affected by the experience, because it not only demands a good connection between all of your chakras, but also an openness of mind that most people aren't ready for.

I find it interesting when people tell me that they are open-minded, or better yet, sexually open-minded, because being open-minded to sex means having an "open door in your mind to sexual experience".

This open-mindedness they talk about is probably not what they claim, as this is what it means. But too many people think they understand things they clearly don't, because they are not spiritually evolved enough to be able to accept certain truths.

You are sexually open-minded when you can surrender your mind to a partner, and allow the flow of energy to circulate between both.

Obviously, when you do this without love, the opposite happens, as the energy circulating turns negative, and brings one downwards, to the realms of hell. When people have sex without love, they predispose themselves to mental illness, depression and lack of self-love. Quite commonly, and not surprisingly, such people also develop suicidal thoughts.

It is all related to their actions, even though many psychologists can't see it, for lack of knowledge on the spiritual side of the individual's nature (the most important one too), reason why they tend to fail in helping these persons, especially women; or, also quite commonly, because they feel that by matching social ideals, they are more likely to profit from the ignorance of others.

Why would professionals of mental health contradict common beliefs when they can profit much more by accepting them?

The Spiritual Consequences of Promiscuity

Too much of what has been normalized has nothing of normal about it. In today's world, it's much more common for women to be promiscuous and have more sexual partners than men, and that's why they tend to suffer more with mental illness and depression.

Men, on the other hand, never suffered from depression for being promiscuous, because their body and mind are not connected in the same way, but are certainly suffering now from lack of love. And because men are not seen as loving creatures, and even they themselves want to be perceived as strong and aggressive, they also suffer alone with their loneliness, which explains the increasing percentage of suicide among the male species.

Men, for being less empathic than women, tend to suffer much less from their sexual experiences with strangers, and that's why the idea of equality in sexual liberation will never match whatsoever people want to be true. A woman is always prostituting herself when having sex with a stranger, and I use this term in a spiritual sense, more than social.

Men, on the other hand, perceive their sexual experiences differently and don't lose so much as women do with each sexual encounter with a stranger.

Now, what I just said may be seen as offensive to many people, brainwashed by the wrong values, but it's the truth. If we want to understand equality, we need to evolve beyond our thoughts and into this truth. Because the real equality between genders is found in the fact that our spirit has no gender.

Nevertheless, the fact that our spirit has no gender, does not make us equal, but bond to different karmic experiences, learned differently due to the differences in how our bodies perceive them.

We all reborn in different bodies, but not always as men or women; and when this process is not properly completed, the spirit degenerates into a homosexual or a transgender. Yes, the word is degeneration, because even though I can respect my homosexual friends, I can only help them by looking at their spirit, not their sexual preferences, and that means helping their soul find love — self-love and the love of someone that can love them in return.

Finding a soulmate then, is not about giving away our body to any sexual encounter but rather to perceive the different encounters we have in their meaning to our spirituality.

A soulmate will present very specific traits, and it's only with such people that sex should occur, and when occurring, with the intention of ending in an everlasting marriage, and not just a casual adventure.

Law 7: Our chakras become blocked whenever sexuality is separated from our emotions, and can only be unblocked with genuine love.

The Meaning of Reincarnation in Our Personal Life

The meaning we should attribute to our reincarnation is hope and the fulfillment of ancient desires.

You can obviously create new relationships and start new emotions with a new person, and you do this with everyone you encounter, but the real meaning in whatever you do, is truly to develop as a spirit and beyond your current self, bringing back the lessons unlearned from the past, while preparing yourself to become a better person for the following future.

Now, when you meet someone you loved before and you love this person again, and freely, this is a great opportunity for you to learn about yourself too, and discover an old side of your eternal spirit, in both its strengths and weaknesses.

With it, comes a renewed sense of what happiness is for you.

For example, when someone tells me that she can't find her life purpose, I always see something else causing this sense of nothingness; because either they have found a soulmate that will guide them there, or they are in a relationship with the wrong person, guiding them in the wrong direction, and making them confused about their real and eternal nature.

A desire with hundreds of years in a spiritual evolution is certainly a strong one, and you cannot ever lose it, as it is alive in you — it is in who you are.

On the other hand, if your soulmate can't recognize this, and notice the obvious joy that he or she feels in your presence, they will lose it, often by getting distracted with the carrots life puts in front of them, as they will follow what their friends or relatives say, or the job opportunities they get to be far from you, exactly like a donkey following a carrot.

They may never get the same chance again also, but you must desire love to get love.

When people can't appreciate what they get, they always lose it, most of the times, distracted by ideas that lead them nowhere.

I have personally been cheated in two relationships with two soulmates, both of which betrayed me with men they believed to match them better, because in one case he was much richer than me, and in another case he matched what she heard from a fortuneteller in what regards the man of her life. And well, these new adventures of them lasted only a few months, before they collapsed.

Then these women tried to come back to me again, without success. But despite all the pain they gave me, when trying to get me back, I have to really be thankful for their departure, for they were too dumb to appreciate me and recognize what I brought to their life. By leaving, they cleared my path to find someone better and to rediscover my true self.

Indeed, we have to be grateful for the idiots who leave us, even if we met them before and need to sadly see them repeating the same dramas for themselves.

Why are People Irresponsible about their Karma

The reason why so many people do dumb mistakes in their life and even claim not to know their life purpose, is fundamentally because they are not connected to their spirit. They see only with the brain they were born with, and in doing so, they see little.

They cannot perceive with their heart, the carrier of their soul, and that's why they allow others to tell them what's good or not good for them.

That's why they allow their beliefs to determine their fate. And when they are then not happy with the outcomes and results, it is only because they allowed themselves to be attached to their personality, which is nothing but a social and cultural construct we molded ourselves into.

If who you are does not match your spirit, you have failed in growing as a person, and you need to restart and relearn how to live; and falling in love is the best opportunity for that.

If it scares you, it's only because you need it more than you think.

You don't have much time to fail and restart again, and again, and again, so you better fail fast.

Never be afraid to change and to ask others to change for you, and to experience life to its fullest.

If you can't love one person, there will always come another; but if you can't love yourself, you can't experience love in its fullest when coming from another person; and you won't find anyone to fulfill that void either.

You must want to love others and be responsible for their emotions towards you, to experience empathy and love in the process. Not many people can love another being, but that's just the way it is, despite the fact that is much harder now.

I have to admit, I often fail on this topic, because it's extremely difficult to feel empathy for someone who is disrespectful, and people these days are too narcissistic to be tolerated. The karmic toll has literally increased.

You should not lose hope just because others are blind about themselves. You must always keep love in your heart, because it can last one lifetime, and even many lifetimes.

Law 8: Whenever you lose your ideal relationship, a void opens to be filled with another, according to your new stage of spiritual development.

How Many Types of Relationship Exist?

Everyone has the right to act and choose according to their own will, and so the questions to ask ourselves are the following:

- Are there many types of relationships?

- And if there are many types, which ones are they?

People may have different opinions, some of which similar, while others apparently distorting reality to delusional levels. This said, they tend to believe that there are certainly many types attached to the idea of a relationship. It's convenient too to believe that, as it allows more space for any personality type to find itself. And for this reason, people tend to become very disappointed when I tell them that there are only two types: Those that work and those that don't.

Do people start relationships not wanting them to work? Let's not consider that for now, but rather focus on the hypothetical fact that they do want their relationships to work.

Like any other decision in life, once we make the decision, such decision itself will change us, and so, without even noticing it, most of the times, people start changing with their relationships and according to the dynamics present in them. And many do believe that you shouldn't change because of another person. However, if you refuse to change, the relationship is still changing you.

You will face more quarrels when refusing to change, and that's a change in itself in the mechanism behind the relationship, as the relationship starts becoming dominated by the motivation for power and control. Which leads us to the next question:

- Who should change?

Whenever people start asking this question to themselves and refusing to change, they are imposing a change on their partner. And well, by doing this, they then initiate a quest for survival inside their own relationship, making it seem like a battleground, in which emotional bombs are constantly thrown at each other.

It's like living with the enemy under the same roof.

This paradox, of being in love with someone we hate, makes many feel that they are in a normal state of being, possibly, due to the many bad movies they watch, written by screenwriters filled with bad views on life, or simply trying to profit from the weaknesses of others. But let us continue here to see furthermore behind this picture: Can we really love and hate at the same time?

When love turns into resentment and resentment diminishes our self-esteem, a relationship moves on to the opposite direction, and will tend to turn inwards. Most of our fights in these cases are not as much about our partner as they are about ourselves.

In fact, I could even say that the story I described you about my soulmate is related to a battle for self-respect on both sides. We both need trust, commitment and love.

These needs are so common, that only karma justifies finding a soulmate to help us solve them. And that is why we can affirm that karma is neither necessarily good or bad. It really depends on what we do with it.

We could also ask ourselves: Can people love one another without self-love?

At one point, they will start comparing their companion with their friends, and may even consider that their friends make them happier. But why would anyone want a relationship that doesn't make them happy?

Well, when people start a relationship that they claim to have been a waste of their time, and then move on to the following one, expecting something to be different, while acting in the same way, they will most commonly repeat the same mistakes. And it will come a day in which such people realize that there's something wrong with them. Or not, as they may never see it.

THE 14 KARMIC LAWS OF LOVE

Frequently, that day never comes, because then they are in their 40s, 50s or 60s, and don't even have the physical attributes anymore that allow them to make proper choices. Their social circle and options are much more scarce now.

Why Most People Can't Change?

If most people do decide to go forward towards a path of change, it should be obvious what kind of changes are needed, for they have repeated the same mistakes multiple times.

In other words, their behavior patterns have led them to repeated experiences. But we must consider which necessary changes we can pick from one relationship, the one we wanted the most to work, and didn't.

Quite often, we make conclusions based on what we think we saw, and commonly, what we see is being filtered by our own thoughts of what should or not be real.

We don't fully see the whole picture of why things happen the way they do.

In any relationship, there is the potential to make it last, and it lasts precisely because there is love. Being ego the opposite of love, only selfishness can destroy a relationship — whenever you focus only in your wants and needs, and expect another person to satisfy them for you.

Until you ask yourself how can you make another person happy, you won't know how love can change you in the right direction. Moreover, a relationship should be based on mutual agreements based on cooperation, a satisfaction of mutual needs.

Taking into consideration that you either have a relationship that works or one that doesn't, we can say that they don't merely serve the purpose of teaching us.

In the ones that work, we will find that plus the experience of feeling loved. But indeed, the two things are always present, so you can learn and also love.

There's no such thing as arriving at a relationship to only love and expect it to magically happen. Our divergences, in values, experiences and insights, guide us to assume different things about our reality, and this becomes even more obvious when addressing our biology and the differences between genders, which, despite much controversy, is a fact.

This leads us to naturally assume that there's only one type of relationship — the one in which love is accepted. The other type is always a refusal from the start.

What people that start their relationships with expectations based on selfish needs are really doing, is going around the relationship itself, thinking that they have one. It would be like putting a soccer player in a soccer field and watching him running around without touching the ball.

The fights that would follow, would be like asking him why is he not touching the ball, while hearing all type of excuses related to everything except touching the ball:

- "Why do you shout at me?";
- "You never give me attention";
- "I expected different things from you".
- "It's your fault for having false expectations on me."
- "You are not patient enough."
- "You don't respect our differences in opinions."
- "Why do you think you know more than me?"
- "I have the right to do whatever I want."

Can you see how the things we say to our partner or listen from the partner are completely ridiculous when compared to any game?

We play the game of life to win, but we should expect our partner to play in our team, and play to win.

This leads us to the obvious fact that people either accept their relationship or reject it. Everything else beyond that is fooling around with facts.

We can see it once we decide to observe, for people say far more truth through their actions than they ever will with their words.

THE 14 KARMIC LAWS OF LOVE

As I said to my last soulmate: "You may think that you want a serious relationship, but you don't behave like you do."

Law 9: You are always changing, either consciously with appreciation, or subconsciously with resentment.

How To Accept Love Between Soulmates?

When you accept love in a relationship, you are accepting the emotions that come with it, and for many people, such emotions conflict with their self-image, reason why they can't be loved.

Beyond that, you have the fear of loving and being betrayed, which means the person expects something that she, herself, can't provide.

If a woman had sex with many partners, for example, she will be more familiar with praise than love. Love, that idea of being connected to someone she has sex with, will feel strange, threatening, and even conflict with her idea of independency.

Why shouldn't it be so? After all, to accept that one man is connected to her would mean accepting that all her sexual adventures were too, and that is a strong blow on the self-esteem of a person.

The same could be said about abandonment. When a woman is abandoned by many partners or, quite simply, has a huge history of failure behind her, she will have more doubts than certainties when starting a new relationship, and will be quicker to judge than to correct her behaviors and deal with misunderstandings.

That is why the more sexual partners people have, the harder it is for them to trust someone with their emotions. And that matters, either we look from the angle of loving someone or receiving love.

Most people only learn about love through movies and books, and such stories are full of drama. Therefore, they place drama in their life, on purpose, in order to test it, and in doing so, they often lose what they were afraid to lose, reinforcing their own fears and false expectations.

Nobody ever got a map about how to find love, so what other options do they have?

Usually, people are familiar with the emotion itself, but they fail in processing the meaning such emotion has for them. And so, they look at their partner for the answer, and like a little child, break him or her in layers, through tests and trials, to see the response, in order to understand what they need.

However, as any professional researcher knows, the result of a research is always determined by the paradigms of the researcher who formulated the questions. In other words, the masses, who understand zero about doing an academic research, test their partners, thinking that such behavior will lead them somewhere. And the only conclusions they get, whatever they are, keep reinforcing their own self-beliefs, their own subconscious patterns, which existed already before they even met the person.

It's very easy for me to identity such patterns in a partner, although I never succeeded in making them reach that level, above the subconscious and conscious mind, called sanity.

Here are some examples I remember vividly and my explanations:

- "Belief: You are aggressive"; Answer: No, your father is aggressive, because he beat your mother all her life, and you grew up with the idea that the same could happen to you, therefore you insulted me every single week, and even attacked me physically, just to see how aggressive I could be. I am not aggressive, but you surely won't quit until you can prove that I am, because you can't accept that I am not, and that's your mental disease;

- "Belief: You don't love me"; Answer: How can you know what love is, if all you did was have sex with strangers and never had any goal of developing a relationship with anyone, much less live with them? Technically speaking, you never loved, so you don't really know what love is either;

- "Belief: You only care about yourself"; Answer: If I don't want my girlfriend to be stupid, and ask her to read, study and learn, and improve her behaviors, especially in public, rather than act like a dumb idiot and flirt with random men, that's caring about the relationship, as much as being selfish would be not to care and do the same, but maybe you're too selfish to understand what empathy is;

- "Belief: You are not ready for a relationship because you can't trust me"; Answer: Why should I trust someone who is flirting every day with different men and doesn't know what she wants? How can I have a relationship with someone who doesn't know what that is and what it implies?

You see, I believe that is easy to love someone who is mentally healthy, but is very hard to love someone who can't love, and is psychologically damaged.

Such people need professional help, even though they tend to lure partners into relationships by preying on the willingness of others to help them, and which typically leads nowhere but a guilt trip for the one who does want to help.

Law 10: Your emotions reflect only your perceptions of reality and not reality itself, because we are always projecting what we can't accept about ourselves.

Understanding Karmic Love Between Soulmates

Right below love, there is compassion, which means to care for someone else's emotions. And below the level of compassion, there is empathy, or the capacity to perceive someone else's emotions. So don't expect someone suffering from Narcissistic Personality Disorder, a Psychopath, or a Sociopath, to be able to recognize all that spectrum of feelings, and much less anything above it.

Once you position yourself from this perspective, you can see that not many people can feel empathy in their relationship, either within themselves or from their partner.

There are many ways people can express their emotions, thoughts and frustrations, but you can indeed resume them to the capacity or not to feel empathy for another person.

This is why to hate the one you love is also a form of empathy. It's actually one that tends to be confused with desire, reason why many tend to feel a stronger attraction in these situations. The two emotions are easily confused because they are both strong emotions confusing our senses.

The best way to understand this and see the potential of a relationship is then based on actions and words deprived from ego. It's when you can do this, that you can truly see if you are loved or not.

How much does the outcome matters to you depends also on how important love is to you and how you see it.

As you don't know when your partner may die, and you don't know also if, for some reason, they may find someone that awakens their deepest desires more strongly, making them forget you ever existed, empathy can then be seen as a form of self-defeat to those who are too arrogant to allow themselves to care for another person. But it's also this type of self-defeat that allows a transmutation towards a more loving soul. And you will know that this transformation is occurring within you, when you start caring more for the feelings of your partner, and even other people.

One of the most interesting experiences for me, was certainly to witness one of my former partners, not only loving me more, but also wanting to love children, have children of her own, and even want to adopt and help homeless dogs. It's interesting because when I met her she told me that she hated children and animals.

That's how much people can change through love.

Obviously, if you want a shortcut into someone's level of empathy and avoid all the drama, you can try to observe their thoughts on children and animals, for that will reveal to you their ability to love a human being, i.e., you.

This is why when people replace one partner for another, they are only fooling themselves, as we are all spiritual beings, and the relationships we have serve to help us evolve faster. Changing partners won't change our nature or our level in that development.

Another great way of knowing if a person loves you, is when that person asks you if you do, because that often means she does not. This is usually reinforced by the choice of words, such as: "Why do you think you love me?"

Well, if that person thinks that love is a process of thoughts, or a conclusive thought, she certainly doesn't understand anything about love. That's why we can confirm that she also doesn't understand what empathy is.

These same people, when asked back why they love, also typically answer in regards the fulfillment of their own needs:

- "You take care of me";
- "You do things for me";
- "You let me do what I want";
- "You cook for me";

- "You want to take me to parties";

- Etc.

They are evaluating love as a currency; the more you do, the higher your GDP. They really don't understand love as an emotional experience.

Some may interpret this as one person loving more than another, but I don't believe in such concept. I believe some people may have higher levels of empathy than others, which makes them more or less capable of loving. But it's very difficult for such empathy levels not to be equalized in a relationship.

To give you an example, simply think about this: How much love does an egotistical Narcissist needs?

I tell you: All you can give. Until you have no more self-esteem and no more sense of peace, and die miserably; or until they find someone else that they consider better than you.

In other words, no amount of love is ever enough for someone that can't love back.

Law 11: Whoever can't feel empathy and express it, can't love himself or others, and is blocked by karma.

The Third Hidden Element in All Relationships

When two persons, obsessed by their needs, meet in a relationship, they can only find lust, because none is willing to love the other.

This emptiness is certainly felt by both at one point, unless they don't care about love, but only their social image, which also is the case for famous celebrities.

What is also interesting about such individuals is that they suffer more from self-hatred than they do about their failed relationships. As they keep on seeking for a partner that can love them more than the previous, and then tend to fail, by not being able to love back, they focus their attention on the wrong things before starting the relationship.

That is why I must tell you that, even though the heart is the symbol for love, the triangle would be a more suitable one. This, because when two persons come together, they tend to forget that the purpose of that bond is to reach a third element, which must be there for the relationship to maintain itself.

That third elements only shows itself in healthy relationships, and not in single lifestyles, or with egotistical souls in a relationship.

The third element is the expression of love, or the emotions that change us — feeling appreciated, wanted, admired, belonged, trusted, hopeful, when with someone else. But is also to have a common goal with another being like raising a family.

It is then normal that couples in love want to have children as the child will represent the physical aspect of that third element — the expression of love between two individuals, and also the resulting investment of their shared emotions, now operating as a vessel, and receiving them directly.

Indeed, the best way a couple expresses love for one another is by loving their own children.

We can also surely say that there are misunderstanding in relationships and many times we can't make the other person understand us. But unless you feel empathy, you can't let go of your assumptions, and try to understand the other person rather than making yourself be understood. For whenever someone can't understand us, we need to hear more and speak less.

It's easy to feel loved when heard, and also easier to reach an agreement when there is love being manifested.

Even though we can say that communication in a relationship is important, it won't work without empathy and trust. And certainly enough, you can't really talk to a liar that has no consideration for your feelings. That's why narcissists can't have normal relationships with anyone — they are liars without empathy.

You can love someone who can't love you back. It's called unilateral love. But you just can't expect to have a normal relationship with such person. It would be like being married to a ghost.

Now, normal people always want to improve themselves and they listen to the needs of their partners, so you should't expect that from someone below that level of mental capacity.

You can't know if someone who decides to go sleep somewhere else is alone or not, if that person violates your trust by not truly caring about how you feel. The same if he or she says that is always thinking about cheating, or flirts with other people, in front of you or behind your back.

That's why trust is the basis of a relationship, but also the main operating mechanism of our society. And this is precisely why relationships do maintain our society at sane levels.

When our society seems too insane, you can trace back the causes to the type of relationships people have.

If you can't find someone willing to love you, then the solution is to be single and love yourself.

THE 14 KARMIC LAWS OF LOVE

You can love yourself by smiling alone and at other people, appreciating your relationship with nature and enjoying doing things alone.

If you are in a difficult relationship, you can simply say to that person: I love you but I can't help you.

If they care, they will put the efforts to make the relationship work. Otherwise, you must learn to let them go.

You are not born to receive but to give, to yourself, to others, to your spouse and the world as a whole. Love is never gone. There is a flow of energy that pulls us towards others, and in certain directions.

If you focus on doing what makes you happy and in spending time with people whose company you enjoy, you will eventually and always find your next partner and the most suitable for you.

If you can remember the teachings of this book, nothing of what you experienced will ever be lost; all teachings and experiences help you grow and become a better human being. And everyone wants a relationship with wonderful loving people, even the worse ones in the world.

Law 12: Life can only expand with trust, empathy and truth.

When and Who Should We Forgive?

The decision to forgive or not someone depends fundamentally on the type of personality in front of you.

There are usually three types of people, each one manifesting different personality traits, although two of these types are more common than others: There is what we call normal, subnormal, and the supernormal. Supernormal people being those who can forgive anyone and under any circumstance.

This type of personality doesn't need forgiveness because they usually don't even hurt others. Their level of empathy is precisely what makes them more caring towards others as well.

They may hurt the insane, but the insane typically don't even know what hurts them. The insane may laugh at those who hurt them and claim to be hunted by those who don't. But that's why they are insane, i.e., they can't tell the difference.

Such was the case with one of my relationships, in which I was complaining about her need to meet one of her friends, who was always making fun of her, trying to break the relationship apart, and basically insulting her with what seemed to be common jokes.

Obviously, this girl had to be either very stupid or very insane to allow that. And yet, she though I was the bad guy, for stopping her from meeting such devilish personalities.

You can't really argue with the insane. They always blame the outcome of their miserable life on someone else, usually the ones who helps them, which is quite insane to do. But what else can you expect from an insane person except insane behaviors?

The strong impulse that such persons have towards their own self-destruction could be labeled as karma. But karma is never as powerful as consciousness. And that is why, the more you understand what karma is, with books like this one, the more you can change it in your favor.

That consciousness does appear, but at an emotional level, rather than mental. Basically, the person understands that something is wrong, and is pushed towards a choice, but not because she understands it.

They could escape karma if the choice was the right one. But most of the times, they don't make the right choice, despite how obvious the choice may seem.

After all, if you have to choose between love and one or two bad friends, you will choose love above bad friendships.

Well, now try to explain this to a delusional soul with a heavy karma, such as with the cases of narcissists, sociopaths and psychopaths?

They typically find themselves reaching the vibration of common sense, when pushed upwards, which is right above resentment, the vibration the insane operate with most of the time. But because they can't be in that vibration, they attack those who love them, pulling themselves back into their own karma.

They are always resentful because they can't take responsibility for their actions. And so, they blame their miserable life on others. And that's also why they keep on being insane.

The insane can be perfectly judged by the levels of responsibility they can assume. Because even if we don't that, karma is doing it to them in this way.

The level above that is basically the capacity to perceive what is normal in society. And insane people struggle quite a lot to reach this level. On the other hand, if the majority of our society acts insanely, that doesn't help much isn't it?

What is known as common sense turns out to be just common insanity; and if you understand common insanity, you can say that you understand common sense; but if the majority is insane, what could then be labeled as insane?

Well, that would have to be the attitude of being negative towards oneself, in a self-destructive way.

Most people aren't insane enough to destroy their own life and relationships, but the insane are. And so, you can forgive two types, but not the insane type.

Who Deserves Love the Most?

The most loving people in the world are the ones I describe here as supernormal.

Supernormal individuals are those who do mistakes by default, and this occurs, because sometimes they want to help too much and end up offending those who are not prepared to be helped.

Sometimes they wish to do too much, and end up stepping on others by accident. Sometimes they want to help too much and talk too much, and can't listen to those talking back to them. And you can forgive them because they never hurt on purpose.

Below this level, there are people trapped in common sense. They do what they observe others doing. And whenever they hurt others, it is simply because they are doing what they observe in others and learn from the media, from the majority around them.

They are like sheep, always following the herd without thinking. And this can be named common sense, until a certain point, until we notice something not so common, which in this case makes us address particular attitudes instead.

We can differentiate what is common through the particular or private attitudes of an individual. More precisely, when someone does what he or she observes others doing, and you complain about the behavior, you are offering a choice: to repeat the behavior or change it; and if the behavior is repeated, you then know that such person is hurting on purpose.

On the other hand, if the behavior is changed, we can say that such person was hurting by default, as in the case of those above these lower levels. But only sane people are capable of correcting their conduct.

Those who can't be forgiven are typically in a vibration of resentment, anger, and hate. Such people can't be forgiven because they are headed for self-destruction, and they will crush everyone on their way too.

They may even use the word love, while the truth is that they love nobody. It's not possible because they can't even love themselves. Their attitude of self-destruction comes precisely from lack of self-love.

Many times society calls them sick, neurotic, psychopathic, narcissistic, and yet, the worse ones among us are very well socially integrated. They have learned to study so well how society operates that they themselves can only be detected in private.

That's why I addressed the gap between private and social behaviors, as the bigger the gap, the worse the case is.

The reasons behind such behaviors comes from a vibration that has been exterior to them. Whenever we absorb such negativity, it often comes in exterior ways.

Those who hurt others on purpose and learn to enjoy that have grown inside insane environments — being abused or seeing others being abused. They have been raised with violence and seeing violence. They learned to normalize violence.

By growing up inside a toxic environment, they learned to mold their personality from within such toxicity, as a mechanism of self-preservation.

Somehow, they learned to associate themselves with physical pain and emotional suffering. They can't forgive their father, or mother, either one is the abuser and the other is the abused, for they started to resent both; they also resent their brothers who couldn't help; and eventually themselves too, for not being able to help.

They then resent the world, their circumstances, the teachers, their bullies in school, etc.

They can't forgive what happens to them, or themselves, and they hold a huge anger within them and towards the world.

This suppressed anger feeds from their energy, and lowers their vibration. And the only way to compensate for this suppressed anger is by diminishing others, by making others feel bad about themselves. That's why they always look for a victim to hurt.

In a way, we can actually say that they are like vampires, seeking for people of a higher energy to literally survive. And those are the ones they often 'fall in love' with.

That is the reason why Christ told us to love our enemies, as when we resent people, we descend to their level, and then grow within that mindset of hate, i.e., hate leads to hate.

The Soulmates You Can't Accept

The personalities who are trapped in hate, are also, due to their vibrational level, more prone to spiritual possession. You can see this right before they get mad, as their eyes change into a predator mode, becoming wide and open as a snake; the facial structure also changes into a more rigid one, because something outside of them, some spiritual force, takes control over their mind through their rage.

Resentment then becomes, through a specific vibratory frequency, the pathway for a spiritual identity to enter at will, and through the emotional tunnel of fear.

I can always predict their attacks by looking at these signs. When they are in a predatory mode, they are not really seeing you, but looking through you.

There are many people in our society who are possessed precisely for these same reasons, as they are immersed in a vibration of hate and resentment, namely, those who try to suppress these emotions.

The majority of the people is ignorant about these things, so the demonic possessed can walk freely in society. However, their vibration is so low, that most of us get frightened in their presence. And, because they know this, whenever they feel threatened, they put a victimhood coat on them, and pretend to be harmless.

The difference and contrast is such that you will feel that you are the crazy one if you see such things.

Such individuals attack more frequently when under the influence of love, because this raises their vibration. And so, that's the moment when the demon interferes, to lower the vibration of the host by attacking the one sharing that energy.

It's a form of vampirism, but the one who is possessed doesn't even notice himself doing such things. And to deny his own insanity or possession, he will then justify his behavior with the reaction of the victim. This, because he can't confront what has just occurred, and is powerless towards his own possession.

They can't be forgiven either because they're lost already. But I'm not saying that all those who suffer become possessed, as everything is relative to the individual and his choices, and even though there is certainly a social trend for spiritual possession.

Law 13: Those who can't forgive and abandon their resentment become trapped in karmic cycles that deny the possibility of being rescued through love.

How Do People Make Themselves Suffer

What happens when people suffer is that they become a kind of hurricane of negativity, and by loving them, others are pulled in and downwards.

This hurricane pulls everything down and dismantles everything and everyone into pieces. Whatever you offer, they nullify and bring it down with irrational justifications and insults.

These individuals are so trapped within their own suffering, their own anger, that they can't feel compassion for anyone and much less be able to process empathy. And whenever we are dealing with someone without empathy, we are dealing with a person that can't process responsibility or think in a normal human way either.

Now, when this happens, you are also dealing with a very dangerous individual. If he is your spouse or colleague, you are exposing yourself to danger.

Those who can't feel empathy, tend to cheat as well, because they can't feel remorse or guilt or shame for their own actions. They feel entitled to what they do and can always find a justification or reason to do it.

The same applies to lying about you to destroy your reputation, steal from you, and literally destroy your capacity to go forward in life.

They are so obsessed with destroying themselves that they can't accept progress in any form either, in a relationship or for themselves alone.

It may seem that they are hard working, but that's only because they value money. Likewise, they may seem very loving when finding a parter that offers them expensive gifts.

They tend to work extra hours in their job if promised a promotion or if they wish to attract someone in the office. Basically, they work to get something in return and not because they like what they do or want to help others.

They can also be very committed in their relationship if something of high value is promised to them.

We all know, for example, that beautiful narcissistic women do anything for money, and many narcissistic men can easily leave their wife to pursue a younger and more attractive woman, and won't leave the marriage if given freewill to cheat.

In essence, we are dealing with someone that can make promises but will never help us create any future. Besides, what you will see is always a cycle repeating itself:

- First, they hurt you on purpose;

- Second, they pretend it wasn't on purpose;

- Third, they repeat what they have done before, but this time accusing you of fault or of deserving the pain;

- Fourth, they use provocation to prove they have the power to control your emotions;

- Fifth, comes the stage of codependency, because you do start feeling like you need their cooperation and agreement to stop the fights that they themselves create. And at that moment in time, if you try to gain back control over the situation, that's when they start showing regret and many times even crying. This, because they are losing you and want to hold you back. But once this repeats, what they are really doing is a kind of showering with compassion that isn't truly there, promises that won't be kept, just to hold you again in the same cycle of insanity.

That's their own nature and they can't change it. The more time you spend with such people, the more they will do this in different forms, the more they will test your weaknesses, the more they will observe you and test you.

They will then hurt you in different ways, to see which ones makes you suffer the most.

They never stop doing this, because they are obsessed with control. This is why they are constantly asking personal questions about your life and personal relationships — they want to know how you think, in order to exercise their control and manipulation over you.

Karma and the Obsession with Manipulation

The obsession over control and manipulation is, quite simply, due to fear of abandonment.

As crazy as it may seem, those who exercise constant control want to destroy you, so that you can't abandon them. And yet, the more devalued you are, the more they seek someone with a higher social value. Because, after all, if you have no value, you can't increase theirs either.

They believe that if you are kept weak with constant emotional abuse, you won't be capable of abandoning them, even if they cheat on you.

As a matter of fact, when your partner starts devaluing you, you can start questioning cheating behaviors. That was what I found to be a constant with the soulmates referred in this book, including the last case.

Such people are incapable of self-analysis and reflection on their behaviors. And the more attention they get, as in the case of very attractive women, the less they feel the need to consider the impact of their actions on others, and the more entitled they feel to hurt.

They never think that they should just not hurt. Instead, they want to keep you locked emotionally while hurting you back. They will never quit doing this and will never stop.

You could believe that we meet evil personalities to make ourselves stronger and better, but there's another problem here, and that's murder by accident. These are the ones that, when driving a car, can cause an accident in which you die. These are the ones who always distort the truth and the facts to make you look bad and stupid. They are the ones who isolate you from your friends by making you look bad in front of them.

They will literally destroy your life and then abandon you when you are a total wreck and completely emotionally dependent on them.

We don't necessarily need to address this topic by mentioning demonic possession furthermore. We can mention personality disorder or even psychiatric characteristics and traits to explain it. But whatsoever is the title you give it, toxic personalities do have a negative vibration and bring others down with their toxicity, and that's why you can't forgive such people or love them.

Having a soulmate in your life is a beautiful experience. But some people are too damaged to experience this type of love with you. You can only love them from the distance, and seek someone else who can love you back.

I hope this book has helped you in this path. Because finding a soulmate and being in a healthy relationship with such individuals is one of the best and most fulfilling life experiences.

That is also why I have no regrets in having met my own soulmates, and despite their very negative karma. I only wish I had been stronger to leave them sooner, and wiser in finding the right person to love.

Law 14: Never volunteer to pay the karmic debts of others or you will attract more negative karma to yourself.

The 14 Karmic Laws of Love

Law 1: We reencounter those who are still emotionally connected to our spirit.

Law 2: The spiritual mechanics guide us beyond our personal will.

Law 3: Karma operates in cycles that repeat themselves if unsolved.

Law 4: We find our soulmate to love again and grow with the experience by putting our

emotions ahead of our social values.

Law 5: If we allow others to influence our decisions, we may pay karma until the end of

our life.

Law 6: You can only solve your karma with moral behavior and ethical decisions

inspired by your heart.

Law 7: Our chakras become blocked whenever sexuality is separated from our

emotions, and can only be unblocked with genuine love.

Law 8: Whenever you lose your ideal relationship, a void opens to be filled with another,

according to your new stage of spiritual development.

Law 9: You are always changing, either consciously with appreciation, or

subconsciously with resentment.

Law 10: Your emotions reflect only your perceptions of reality and not reality itself,

because we are always projecting what we can't accept about ourselves.

Law 11: Whoever can't feel empathy and express it, can't love himself or others, and is

blocked by karma.

Law 12: Life can only expand with trust, empathy and truth.

Law 13: Those who can't forgive and abandon their resentment become trapped in

karmic cycles that deny the possibility of being rescued through love.

Law 14: Never volunteer to pay the karmic debts of others or you will attract more negative karma to yourself.

About the Publisher

This book was published by the 22 Lions Bookstore. For more books like this visit www.22Lions.com.
Join us on social media at:
Fb.com/22Lions;
Twitter.com/22lionsbookshop;
Instagram.com/22lionsbookshop;
Pinterest.com/22LionsBookshop.

www.ingramcontent.com/pod-product-compliance
Lightning Source LLC
Chambersburg PA
CBHW070613010526
44118CB00012B/1496